HORSE SENSE FOR PEOPLE

MONTY ROBERTS has been working with horses for more than fifty years. He lives on the central coast of California with his wife, Pat, on their major thoroughbred horse farm.

HORSE SENSE FOR PEOPLE

MONTY ROBERTS

HarperCollins*Publishers*

HarperCollins*Publishers*
77–85 Fulham Palace Road,
Hammersmith, London W6 8JB

www.**fire**and**water**.com

First published by HarperCollins*Publishers* as
Join-Up: Horse Sense for People in 2000
1 3 5 7 9 8 6 4 2

Copyright © Monty Roberts 2000, 2001

The Author asserts the moral right to
be identified as the author of this work

A catalogue record for this book
is available from the British Library

ISBN 0 00 653161 X

Set in Stempel Garamond

Printed and bound in Great Britain by
Clays Ltd, St Ives plc

*To those thousands of people who have
come to me and said "You must give us the human
version of the concept of Join-Up."*

LIST OF ILLUSTRATIONS

Monty and Pat riding above Flag is Up Farms, photograph © John
  G. Zimmerman, first published in *California* magazine
Monty working as a camp counsellor at Douglas Summer Camp,
  © Delmar Watson Photography
Monty and Pat releasing the first horses at Flag is Up Farms
Roberts family © 1967, Los Angeles Times Photo
Marty and Monty © Monty and Pat Roberts, Inc
The wedding of Steve and Sherry Arellano, photograph © George
  Ives, Solvang
Monty with grandson Matthew © Monty and Pat Roberts, Inc
Monty and Pat at home © Monty and Pat Roberts, Inc
Monty and Shy Boy © Monty and Pat Roberts, Inc
The audience at a demonstration of Join-Up in Australia © Monty
  and Pat Roberts, Inc
The blind trust walk © Monty and Pat Roberts, Inc
A talk at a Border's book signing © Monty and Pat Roberts, Inc
Monty chatting to readers at a bookshop in Australia © Monty and
  Pat Roberts, Inc
Monty with a youthful horse lover © Monty and Pat Roberts, Inc
A young physically challenged student is encouraged by Monty ©
  Monty and Pat Roberts, Inc
Monty with a young friend © Monty and Pat Roberts, Inc
John Newton from Exxon © Monty and Pat Roberts, Inc
Monty and Pat enjoying a dance together © Monty and Pat
  Roberts, Inc
Monty waiting to enter the arena, photograph by Michael
  Schwartz, © Monty and Pat Roberts, Inc
Monty lecturing a group of students © Monty and Pat Roberts, Inc
Monty at a radio broadcasting studio © Monty and Pat Roberts,
  Inc
A young fan meeting Monty © Monty and Pat Roberts, Inc
A corporate group in the round pen © Monty and Pat Roberts, Inc
Clay Smith on Cadet and Jake Smith on Shy Boy © Monty and Pat
  Roberts, Inc

FOREWORDS

It took almost my business lifetime to begin to understand the tremendous power that can be leveraged when people's individualism, creativity and wisdom are unleashed.

In recent years there has been a growing appreciation of enlightened forms of leadership that seek to engage, involve and inspire, as opposed to the long-standing practices of "direct and control."

Meeting Monty Roberts and absorbing his philosophy was a really magical moment for me—I am inspired by his beliefs and impressed by his actions. He clearly demonstrates that kindness and respect for the horse are superior to the traditional breaking of the animal's spirit. Monty's notion that the teacher (or leader) must create an environment in which the student can learn and grow is simple, direct and honest—it fit perfectly with a style of leadership that I have been experimenting with since the early eighties.

Monty Roberts certainly listens to horses but, in my humble opinion, he delivers a powerful message to people and, in particular, people at all levels of leadership. What he achieves with a horse is a metaphor for a style of management—employees will produce exceptional results if they are treated with dignity, respect and honesty.

In the world of organizations and business we make the mistake of putting people in boxes and limiting their abilities and creativity—we need to find a means of changing the way people think about themselves, their jobs and how they work as individuals and in teams. I suggest you couldn't start anywhere better than this book.

CLIVE WARRILOW
Volkswagen North America
CEO and President

I am not usually to be found kicking up the sawdust of a riding ring, especially if it means taking a long drive to get there. My encounters with horses have been limited to having them step on my feet on hot summer camp mornings nearly forty years ago. As an adult, I look at them as not much more than a one-horse power motorcycle with a mind for unpredictability. I once spent a ludicrous amount of money to ride a horse named "Cheesehead" while I looked, dry-mouthed, down a thousand-foot drop in Yosemite National Park convinced that my mount was more interested in biting the rear end of the horse in front of me than concentrating on his footing. I have never grasped why so many people, including gaggles of little girls, have such a big thing for these creatures of tonnage that can decide to run like a demented rabbit just because a piece of paper blows across the trail.

So again, I wonder why I am standing in sawdust while people with big shiny belt buckles, jeans and pointy boots mill around me. The loudspeakers are playing full orchestral renditions of "Don't Fence Me In" and "Tumbling Tumble Weeds." With my nondescript beige pants (khakis?) and T-shirt I must look out of place. I am also too fat to ride horses. I'm surrounded by opposites, hundreds of gangly men and tiny women. Like the horse they appear to love so deeply, they are a different species.

Oddly enough we are all here to see the only other person in the place who doesn't look like he ever rides a horse, Monty Roberts. I'm here to see a man who deciphered the horse's natural language, Equus. By demonstrating its application he is spreading the word about how to rid the world of outmoded concepts about the violent domination of horses. I rather suspect he has simply invented a way to convince a horse that it is in its best interest to allow itself to be ridden. Sure, he is kind of a Jane Goodall or Dian Fossey of the horse world, but I would just as soon watch that kind of thing on PBS.

Why am I here? Why has his best-selling book *The Man Who Listens to Horses* been read by millions of people like me who would just as soon never deal with a horse? The music stops and Monty walks into a circular metal fenced ring. He looks like a London cabby. This is the man who was a child prodigy, a wonder rider. Arguably he knows more about horses than any other person on this earth. His eyes are pale and full of life; yet ironically he is completely color-blind. At sixty-one he has the clarity and cadence of voice of a thirty-year-old. He's not wearing a cowboy hat. There's no denim, just a nondescript jacket.

This is the man who listens to horses. For his first act, he takes a horse that has never been ridden. He communicates with it by using a fascinating body language, all the while talking on a wireless to a hushed crowd. The horse moves nervously around the ring while he allows it, he tells us, to go the usual distance it would if a predator were trying to chase it down. Monty freely admits that he is the predator and gently induces a little anxiety that puts the horse into a trotting flight around the ring. Then Monty does his magic.

The Join-Up begins. Through a series of bossy postures and motions he actually communicates to the horse in Equus and the horse has an amazing change of heart: Monty is not a predator— Monty is now not only a friend, but a powerful one with experience and savvy, offering protection and companionship. The worst fear of every prey herd animal is isolation. Monty has taken advantage of this fear. Within twenty minutes not only has Monty communicated that he isn't a retractable-clawed killing machine, but that he is an in-the-know, all-protective alpha partner. The horse, now "joined-up" with Monty, shows some apprehension if separated from him, like a two-year-old human child trying to keep constant contact with a parent.

Monty's communication with this animal creates a trust that is astonishing. Before the demonstration I sarcastically made the comment to my wife that Monty will probably be taming the most ludicrous of vaudeville beasts. I was overwhelmed to observe just the opposite. His new friend accepts a saddle and a rider, all because Monty said "trust me" in the horse's language. Monty transformed himself from the predator to the horse's ally. Now that horse will go to extremes to comply with him.

During the entire process, Monty has been giving a verbal rundown of what he is doing, even at one point asking the crowd to applaud loudly. It is apparent that Monty has harnessed the horse's willingness to work with him. Every time the crowd applauds, the horse draws itself closer to the man, seeking the safety of its newfound protector. When the applause ends, the horse relaxes, feels free to wander a bit, but still is attentive to Monty's presence. Restarting the applause sends the horse back to Monty for comfort and solace. Monty is clearly perceived as a place of safety. All this is opposite of the age-old practice of breaking a horse, which usually involves inflicting pain and terror on the animal. The traditional method of breaking literally mortifies a horse until it seems to accept its own spiritual death, and in doing so survives.

The real reason I am here is to see a man who is taking a giant leap of faith, past the world of horses. It is simply stated: cooperation is better than domination; the world could use much less pain and fear. Monty has used his knowledge of horses as a vehicle for the message. I see him as a kind of Buddhist monk, who I suspect doesn't even know that he is a practitioner of compassion and empathy in all affairs among people and between people and animals.

I am no "new age" adherent. Too many "new ages" have come and gone for me to be impressed. Today's atmosphere has allowed Monty Roberts to rise to recognition in an arena where men are men and horses are horses, and this is good. He is as much a reflection of the times as the other way around.

It is a simple, if large, step from a new kind of relationship between person and animal to learning to take the time to understand the ground on which all other people and living things stand. We are the truly pliable ones. If we want to talk to turtles, then it is up to us to learn turtle language, not the other way around.

Monty Roberts has demonstrated that all relationships can be based on a spirit of cooperation and empathy, whether it is with a ferret or the entire biosphere. All that is required is that we take the time and have the patience to learn the other's language instead of brashly imposing our own. We are the capable ones. Primate researchers spent years trying to teach a chimpanzee to talk. All that came of it was a desperate ape that could barely say "mama." Then our behavioral experts started to lighten up and stopped insisting on our way of doing things; before long chimps were babbling away using sign language. Their brains don't have the motor control that allows the complexities of human speech.

Monty takes obvious pride in breaking a long chain of violent human domination. His message is clear and simple: all violence is bad; cooperation is good. There will always be conflicts in nature. It's the way of the world. There are distinctions. Man's violence against man is virtually always immoral. Nature is always amoral. My message is simple: I went to see Monty Roberts and watched him work with two horses. I learned about the language of Equus. I still don't like the beasts and probably won't again see the inside of a riding ring for years to come, but I did see a happy man who loves people, and who, while staying within the realm of horses, managed to plead for quietus, peace and compassion between people and the animals with which we cohabit this blue-green sphere. Equus is just the first language. There are many, many to come if we only take the time to stop, look, listen and Join-Up.

MICHAEL SCHWARTZ, PH.D.
Prime Factors Inc.
Chairman

ACKNOWLEDGMENTS

As with everything that I do in life my first debt of gratitude is to the horses. Thousands of them contributed to my learning process but Ginger, Brownie, Johnny Tivio, Dually and Shy Boy are the cornerstones.

In an effort to cover Join-Up comprehensively I have surrounded myself with a team of very good advisers. I call them farmers for their ability to plough the fields of my mind and there plant seeds. At the outset, I took on two farm foremen: Dr. M. B. (Flip) Flippen, who works in the fields of education, and Marc Bridgham, from Boeing, who helped me understand the corporate world better.

M. B. "Flip" Flippen, founder and president of M. B. Flippen & Associates, has one mission: to make a difference. For over twenty-five years Flip has been in the business of seeking practical solutions in the field of education and then empowering people to implement them. He has assisted me and essentially verified that my concepts can be used for humans as well as horses. His influence on me can be traced throughout these pages. We have spent many hours together as he inspired me to realize that education, whether of horses or humans, is the foundation of our existence.

Many hundreds of people have shared their powerful experiences and brought me intellectual information. Dr. William R. Miller, of the Department of Psychology and Center on Alcoholism, Substance Abuse and Addictions (CASAA), University of New Mexico, spread a ton of seed in the meadows of my mind, which have taken root and found a place in these pages. My deepest thanks go out to Dr. Miller for looking over my shoulder during the creation of this book.

Bob Foxworthy, of Foxworthy Corporate Consultants, gave me encouragement and the validation needed to go forward with confidence. Bob's team takes my concepts to the corporate world.

The Innovation Network, with Joyce Wycoff and Andrea Woodward, gathered together people from all over the world and helped to explore the principles included in this book.

Special recognition has to go to Michael Schwartz, who joined the team and assisted, contributing immeasurably to the final product.

Any words that I use to thank Clive Warrilow, CEO of Volkswagen North America, for his generosity are woefully inadequate. Mr. Warrilow reached out to allow the readers of this book to benefit by agreeing to the use of one of his speeches.

I was blessed with the encouragement and knowledge of the team from Manchester Business School, Manchester, England, led by its director, Professor John Arnold. Sylvia Arnold originally introduced the institution to my work and it has been very supportive.

From the world of publishing I find that I continue to rely heavily on the advice of Louise Dennys, Knopf, Canada, which has published each of my three books. Her knowledge and generosity have been a primary factor in whatever success these books have had. Molly Stern, my editor at Viking, New York, is a new acquaintance who has enthusiastically taken up the challenge of assisting me in producing this book. Molly and Louise are a team that turned out to be essential in getting me the right book. They deserve my heartfelt thanks. Barbara Fisher and Elmar Klupsch, Lubbe, Germany, have proven to be an invaluable team from the very beginning.

Jane Turnbull, my literary agent in London, has been with me from the very start and has worked tirelessly to make sure my books reach as many people as possible.

The list of those individuals who have encouraged and assisted me would literally number tens of thousands. Those students and attendees who have directly contributed to, or asked me for, this book are deeply appreciated by me.

Crawford Hall and his team at the Monty Roberts International Learning Center made a valuable contribution. My son Marty is in charge of the farm and our business operations and through his efforts I have been allowed the time to create this book.

My critics should be acknowledged because they caused me to get up early every morning and work hard on my skills, and without criticism there is really no reason to advance one's concepts.

Caroline Baldock, my literary assistant, has quite possibly put in more hours on this book than all of the rest of us put together. Caroline believed in it from the very beginning and encouraged me in those times when I wanted to walk away from it. Caroline worked at Flag Is Up, but also in England and Germany, and even logged many hours somewhere over the North Pole. Her energy, dedication, loyalty and grit are unmatched by anyone with whom I have worked.

Last, but most important, my wife Pat came forward to assist me at all stages of organizing this book in a way that no other human being could. Pat and I have now been married for forty-three years and there is simply no one who knows me or my work as well as she does. This enables her to advise me on virtually every aspect of my philosophy. Pat spent countless hours at home and on demonstration tours reading and suggesting improvements to this book.

CONTENTS

One

JOIN-UP: THE JOURNEY

1

Two
COMMUNICATION
32

Three
AGAINST VIOLENCE
67

Four
TRUST
83

Five
RESPECT
124

Six
THE GOOD PARENT
148

Seven
CHOICE
174

Eight
CHANGE
189

CONCLUSION
206

MONTY ROBERTS'S
IDEAS TO LIVE BY

A good trainer can hear a horse speak to him.
A great trainer can hear a horse whisper.

Many people watch, but few see.

If your horse wants to go away, don't send it
away a little, send it away a lot.

Make it easy for him to do right and
difficult for him to do wrong.

Always work to cause your horse to follow the path of
least resistance. Then place an opening for him to pass
through so that the path of least resistance becomes the
direction you want him to go in.

It is not the great trainer who can cause his horse to perform.
The great trainer can cause a horse to want to perform.

Violence is for the violator, never the victim.

There is no such thing as teaching, only learning.

Everyone has the right to fail.

No guts, no gain.

It is a teacher's duty to create an environment
in which the student can learn.

If he is about to learn, stay out of his way.
If all learning is zero through ten, then the most
important part of learning is zero through one.

Everyone must be responsible for their own actions
and the consequences thereof.

No blade of grass has ever run from a horse.
Do not use food as a reward.

No one has the right to say you must!

The horses are talking . . . just listen.

*The horse is the quintessential flight animal.
When pressure is applied to the relationship, he will almost
always choose to flee rather than fight.*

*A horse trainer must keep in mind the idea that the horse can
do no wrong; that any action taken by the horse, especially
the young unstarted horse, was most likely influenced by him.*

*The horse uses a predictable, discernible and effective
language. Their language, which I call Equus, is nonverbal.*

*The most important piece of equipment in horse training is
the hands that hold the reins. Equus has been my teacher, my
friend and my provider; he can be yours.*

Keep it simple. Simple is best.

FROM HORSES TO HUMANS
My Philosophy of Join-Up

You can lead a horse to water, but
you can't make him drink.
—ANON

•

You can lead a man to knowledge,
but you can't make him think.
—JERRI SHINNAMAN

I suppose all readers of this book have the right to ask what gives me the authority to expound my theories on human-to-human communication. To many people, my only claim to fame, if there is one, is as a horse psychologist. As I write this book, it is my sincere hope that I will give the reader the understanding that there is a balance between all living beings on this earth and that we are all one family. If my work only brings to light certain limited connections between human and horse, then I am very disappointed. Humankind has the most complex brain of any species on earth, and with such incredible cerebral power we must be able to apply what we learn from animals to ourselves.

The first book in which I wrote about my ideas was *The Man Who Listens to Horses*, published in 1996. In 1989 I had been invited to demonstrate my training methods to Her Majesty Queen Elizabeth II. Since my methods break with tradition it seemed to be a refreshing sight to her to watch me cause untrained horses to calmly accept their first saddle, bridle and rider in about half an hour, although traditional methods take four to six weeks. Possibly even more intriguing was the fact that I used no pain or restraint, even though the methods used for approximately 8,000 years have been loaded with both those elements.

The queen was curious as to how I had learned these things and what had brought me to the conclusions that are now the basis of my work. She encouraged me to write a book chronicling my concepts. The prospect was daunting, since I'd never viewed myself as a writer. Approximately six months later I returned to England to work with some of the royal horses and hoped that the queen had forgotten about my writing a book. Not so! One of her first questions concerned my literary efforts and progress to date. I resigned myself to producing the story of my life.

Since that life is chronicled in *The Man Who Listens to Horses*, I will only touch on it here.

I was born in 1935 to parents who were in the horse business. My father was a trainer and riding instructor who had an agreement with the city of Salinas, California, to manage its competition grounds. This was a large equestrian facility and home to one of the major rodeos in the United States. I was up on a horse with my mother shortly after my birth and was in competition when I was four years of age.

Traditional trainers worked on the principle, "You do what I tell you or I'll hurt you." As I grew up I came to the conclusion that it is far more effective to wait for horses to do something right and reward them. I began to experiment with training techniques that disciplined the horse by putting him back to work, never by applying force. I refused to inflict pain of any kind. I believed that horses, these wonderful flight animals with no agenda to cause harm to anyone, could teach us that violence is never the answer.

Throughout my career, horses have been my allies and they have done the talking for me. Champion after champion came my way, both in the show ring and on the racetracks of the world. The raising of three biological children and dozens of foster children educated me further in the concepts that the horses were so freely, by their example, communicating. I've spent many years now working with horses to communicate those same concepts to people as individuals, in the family and in the workplace.

On tour, I do demonstrations of my work, using horses I have never seen before. At these events I sign books and answer questions from attendees. One of the most frequent requests has been that I should produce a book that relates my concepts to humans. This book is my attempt to answer the call of literally millions of people around the world to extend the concepts of Join-Up and nonviolence to people.

Fundamental to my development of what I have termed Join-Up—a nonviolent method of communicating to establish a partnership with a horse—was an early recognition that the horse must always be allowed the freedom to choose whether or not he will cooperate. It seemed to me, as I watched my father and other traditional horse trainers work, that their entire focus was on telling the horse that he had no choice. Pain is not a choice any healthy being makes, and inflicting pain forces the horse to understand that absolute obedience is the only choice. Pain can achieve obedience and compliance, but I believe that compliance alone is not sufficient for outstanding performance. Blind obedience is not pleasurable nor does it produce a sense of accomplishment.

Communication with horses in Join-Up is largely based on the fact that they are flight animals. Using the horses' language I proceed one step at a time and respect their natural patterns of behavior. I understand their desire to flee from what they perceive as danger and, going along with their natural instinct, I ask for and offer respect. The horse is then left to make the willing decision to Join-Up with me.

This idea of choice is one of the root principles of my work. *No one* has the right to say, "You must or I will hurt you," to any creature, animal or human.

These concepts of nonviolence, respect and choice are important and can be equally effective in the human arena. Join-Up allows us to see and understand that violence and confrontation are never the answer. When observing, for example, how organizations often recruit and train new employees I often see similarities to the traditional method of breaking a horse. We need to realize that a harmonious partnership in the workplace, in the family or in any other social context is far more productive than one of force and intimidation.

When it comes to the crucial question of choice, there is yet another similarity between human-to-horse partnerships and human-to-human partnerships. If I have been at all successful, I must attribute much of the credit to my early recognition that when we partner with a horse we are asking him to do things that are threatening and against his very nature. To saddle a horse, for example, is to provoke the sense that he is being attacked by a predator and this leads him to act in self-defense. To inflict pain for behavior that is a natural response simply confirms the horse's fears. Yet books on traditional horsemanship consistently recommend whipping the horse when it acts out against its first saddle. I searched instead for ways to communicate to the horse that choosing to accept tack and equipment was a reasonable decision. I realized that I had to communicate to the horses that they could trust me, and I had to earn that trust. I found, time and again, that I could cause the horse to discover the joys of working together, all without coercion and pain.

Let's face it—in most work situations, we are asking humans to make choices that are equally unnatural, equally threatening. Considerable conditioning is required before we can live by a regimented schedule or sit and perform repetitive motions for long periods of time. It is not natural to follow a rigid set of rules and guidelines and to have our security and future in the hands of people we don't know or perhaps even like. This is not what the human body and mind are naturally equipped to do. Many of the behaviors employees resent in employers are simply the result of natural resistance to unnatural conditions. One of the goals in human-to-human Join-Up, then, is to create, through communication and behavior, situations where the satisfaction of cooperation outweighs the negative reaction to unnatural conditions.

This search for ways to create partnership and healthy choices is more complicated in the human world. Humans can either be fight or flight animals: because of our make-up, we are constantly deciding whether we are predator or prey, whether flight or confrontation is the most prudent course. This dynamic is ever present in both our personal lives and the workplace. We usually don't have to fear being eaten, but we face many other threats.

An easy way to test this is to observe your physical and emotional reaction the next time you are told unexpectedly that the boss wants to see you in his office. You are likely to find yourself immediately in fight or flight mode. This response has long been understood in the study of human stress. By providing a third alternative, i.e., "partnership," Join-Up creates a way out of the dilemma.

At first glance what I do with a horse in the round pen (the structure in which I work with the horses) may seem miles away from the complex interactions that occur between people, but the parallels are closer than most people think and encompass the full gamut of human existence, from political parties to classrooms and even families.

There is a constant struggle between the need to be an individual and the need to belong to a group. Both needs are natural and healthy, but the struggle between them is at the heart of much of the difficulty of organizational, family and social life. We want to be an individual, but we resist being isolated. Our relationship and commitment to work is a constantly moving tension between engagement and disengagement. Experiences either draw us in or push us away. They either create resistance, which results in fighting or fleeing, or they create commitment and collaboration.

I could easily have written two books—one relating what I've learned from horses and applying it to life in the workplace and management practices and another book on how those lessons shed light on personal and family relationships. Ultimately I believe we live one life—our lives aren't separated off into "nine to five" or "five to nine." We carry the emotional baggage of the one to the other. In this book I want to stress that what we are in the one flows straight into the other, and although too many of us are now apt to forget it, five to nine is just as important as nine to five. If our relationships with our husbands or wives, our parents or children are fractured or unsatisfactory, of course we carry those worries and problems through our working day; and we all know we take the dissatisfactions and anger of the day home at night.

While the violence dealt out by man to horses is largely physical violence, human beings have many ways of exhibiting violence, which can be as harmful and pernicious: verbal abuse, which may involve belittling, or dismissiveness or threats, can be as crippling to the human spirit. Human beings too often use physical violence, but verbal abuse is also a common tool of those in positions of authority—parents or employers, for example. Man has spent many years of his relationship with horses trying to dominate them. There is a potential danger of violence whenever a relationship involves a dominant partner and a weaker partner, whether in emotional family situations or in the workplace. Such dominance can be one of physical power, gender, age, social position, work hierarchy, wealth or race, but wherever it is found it all comes down to one human being saying "you must" to another.

By acknowledging the power of people to choose, and by learning to communicate without coercion, the philosophy of Join-Up provides a way to resolve tension and struggle. By presenting the invitation and by freely allowing people to make choices as to how to be, we honor them and allow them to fulfill themselves and their role and responsibilities of Join-Up; we honor both needs.

There is, however, one striking difference between human-to-horse and human-to-human Join-Up and it concerns this matter and the difference between compliance and commitment by choice. When I work with horses, I ask them to make choices about cooperation: whether or not to be saddled and ridden, for example. When our work is finished, the horse is essentially free to be himself—he is free of the responsibilities and commitment I asked of him. But for an organization to be successful, we depend on groups of people making the right choices even when they are on their own, just as we also depend on our children learning to make right choices when on their own.

As a person sits in his or her cubicle or office, or works on the line or in the field, it is his or her right to decide how much energy to put forth, how much brainpower to engage or how much attention to pay to detail. The difference between compliance and commitment is the difference between making the choice to do just enough to get by, and doing enough to excel.

•

I have long believed that the essence of what happens in the Join-Up process with horses is equally valid when initiating and sustaining human relationships. But even I, at my most optimistic, was hardly prepared for the level of interest that my ideas would generate outside the horse world.

Men and women, young and old, would line up for hours after a public demonstration to reveal to me how what they had seen reflected their own personal lives, or how they had learned, through my book *The Man Who Listens to Horses*, to confront and deal with abuse or violence in their lives.

Among those who attend my demonstrations or visit Flag Is Up Farms are a significant number of executives, business consultants and leaders from major institutions. In working with these leaders I have discovered an almost unbelievable hunger for better ways to work together.

There seems to be a tide of change sweeping through the world of human institutions that touches all groups of people: schools, prisons, political structures, even the military. The direction of these changes mirrors in a striking fashion my own experiences in Join-Up, and I believe this is why many people who have no interest in horses have read my books and come to me for advice.

When my horse-trainer father attempted to impress upon me, as a small boy, that "horses are dangerous machines," he could easily have been a CEO saying the same thing about his workforce. The idea that horses are wild, obstinate beasts that must be broken into submission is remarkably similar to the way managers have regarded workers over the years: often as the enemy, to be kept under control at all times, or as expendable parts of a machine.

Slowly we are coming to realize that such treatment of humans is archaic and counterproductive. Similarly, there is a growing acceptance in my world that horses will not intentionally hurt you unless you hurt them first. They deserve respect and gentleness and will respond more effectively without violence. The corporate world is slowly confirming that humans want to make a significant contribution in their collaborative endeavors. People want to be good, and if treated with respect, will rise to levels of performance beyond that which they themselves thought possible.

Based on my observations and conversations with leaders, consultants and human resource professionals, I believe that Join-Up has stimulated interest because it is in many ways the logical and full extension of this change in attitude. What I offer in human-to-horse Join-Up is a disciplined but gentle approach to obtaining willing cooperation, which gives profound respect to the "other." Join-Up brings to the table the very real possibility that we can banish the notion of domination and the resulting subservience.

In the early days I found it frightening when I began dealing with the complicated human mind. During the publishing of my first book individuals in the literary world warned me that I might be attacked by the fraternity of psychologists. I remember at those first book signings anticipating with terror the psychologists and psychiatrists who might show up and say that my theories were unacceptable.

Now the strongest supporters of my belief that what the horses have taught me can be applied to human beings are the psychologists and psychiatrists. In letters, debates and discussions I have heard the voices of these professionals louder and clearer than those of any other group requesting this human-to-human book. In writing the book, I've accepted the responsibility to explore the human benefits of what my work has taught me. If you believe, as I do, that people are extraordinary creatures who deserve respect always, and if you are committed to or willing to consider taking that stance, then we can, together, explore the potential of Join-Up in the human arena.

I have been tempted over and over again to create a book that has the following words on each page.

VIOLENCE IS NEVER THE ANSWER.

VIOLENCE IS ALWAYS FOR THE VIOLATOR
AND NEVER FOR THE VICTIM.

IT IS MY BELIEF THAT NO ONE OF US
WAS BORN WITH THE RIGHT TO SAY "YOU MUST
OR I'LL HURT YOU" TO ANY OTHER
CREATURE, ANIMAL OR HUMAN.

Naturally, such a book would not be very well received, so I've held myself back—I've given it to you only in the epigraph at the front of this book and repeated it once more. The truth is, however, that if I could cause every reader to understand, believe in and act on these forty-five words, it would be, in my opinion, one of the most important books ever written.

I could easily expand this message by adding two words: "choice" and "trust." If we give everyone we come in contact with the freedom to choose an outcome while encouraging him to be aware of his responsibilities, then he will learn to make better choices, and if we earn trust and accept our responsibilities, then we take a giant step toward creating successful relationships. Removing responsibility and tightening control directly reduce the learning process. If we trust others because we have caused them to trust us we have completed the circle necessary for exemplary communication.

HORSE SENSE FOR PEOPLE

One
JOIN-UP: THE JOURNEY

The horse has an important message
for humankind

I cannot imagine my life without horses. They have been my teachers, my friends, my business partners and my entertainment. Their message to me has been so strong that I have dedicated my life to interpreting what they are trying to tell us.

When as a boy, I first watched the wild horses out on the Nevada desert, I was immediately surprised by the fact that there was a clearly defined language that they used. I was further surprised by the realization that it was a silent language, one of gestures, much like signing for the deaf. A horse squared up to another, rigid and on point with eyes directed onto the eyes of his subject, is saying, "go away." The positioning of their ears indicates the direction of their attention. Turning to a forty-five degree angle is saying, "You are welcome back into the herd." All the many motions and gestures of the horse add up to a sizeable dictionary of signs and actions.

Later I became a trainer of horses, and over many years developed a set of training principles. The horses I work with are usually "raw," untrained horses or remedial horses that have been physically or psychologically abused. I often meet the horse I am to work with for the first time in a Join-Up session. Join-Up is a consistent set of principles using the horse's own language and designed to let the horse know that he has freedom of choice. I release the horse at the beginning of each session of communication, encouraging him to leave me, therefore exercising his right to flee in order to protect himself. I then encourage him to go away, in essence suggesting that he can do anything he wants. I require him to be responsible for his own actions and for their consequences. I continue to communicate that I will be responsible for my actions, too.

I came to call the process based on these principles or concepts, Join-Up. Fundamental to the process and its remarkable success is my belief in the effective importance of nonviolence and trust.

A STORY

The Mustang Mare

People often ask me if horses are capable of such traits as loyalty, trust, care and concern for other species. I am asked during each "question and answer" session during my demonstrations if I believe that horses possess a sense of caring regarding people. Many academics inquire of me whether or not I truly believe that there could be an interspecies understanding.

My stock answer is that horses live within a social order that is based on the principles of trust, loyalty and mutual concern. I go on to say that they have taught me that without these attributes they could never have existed for their fifty million years.

I don't know that any of us will ever be certain about how much horses actually feel a sense of loyalty toward human beings. I am not sure if anybody will ever know if there is a deep caring or concern on their part for our well-being. I only know what I have experienced with horses and it is with that background that I bring you a story that to me dramatizes these characteristics.

I feel it is quite possible that the story I am about to relate is one of the most important episodes of interspecies communication ever witnessed. I know the importance that this story has for all my work subsequent to its occurrence. I know firsthand the hundreds of horses that experienced a deeper understanding from me because of this experience.

If horses are capable of demonstrating this cross-species care and concern, then how many species are there on earth that have this capability? I feel that many animal behaviorists at work today would ratify my findings with experiences of their own. It seems strange to me that humans find it so difficult to comprehend this.

Each horse in the herd lives by the laws of absolute allegiance. A stallion is loyal and protective of his mares. I have learned about it from horses and I can attest to the fact that breaches of loyalty are far more frequent in the human spectrum than in the equine world. I am not sure if it is a function of their fifty million years of survival of the fittest or whether it is a conscious effort at the moment.

Over the many years that I have been utilizing Join-Up and developing its potential, I have encountered many interesting and sometimes surprising reactions. Each of these experiences allows me a further insight into the power of developing trust. As I go through the process of Join-Up I am engaging in a dialogue with the horse in exactly the same way I hold a conversation with a person. Our conversation creates that basis of trust. I carefully observe the horse as I work with it, assessing its responses to me and the environment it is now in.

We often make false assumptions about people and horses; it is our nature. I have done it in the past and from time to time still do. This story is a reminder of just how wrong we can be and how important it is to make correct and unbiased assessments of people and situations. Our ability to read other people's body language is innate, but sometimes we can even get that wrong. This incident has led me to a greater understanding of the depth of the bond I make with the horse. This experience has brought home to me how deep maternal instincts run in most mammalian species. To my personal knowledge this is the first interaction of its kind. To think that this adult female horse as wild as a deer could so quickly adopt me and move to protect me was overwhelming. It would have surprised me greatly if a domestic mare had reacted in such a fashion. I now realize that it is more likely for the wild one to express this phenomenon because she is so much more acutely aware of the dangers in nature. Subsequent to the incident I have been much more confident when discussing interspecies communication than I was before. This mustang mare proved to me beyond any shadow of a doubt that there is a close interspecies connection most people have failed to observe or experience.

I received a call one day from a lady who had just adopted a mustang mare from the Bureau of Land Management. The mare had a foal at her side, which was not uncommon. The owner had heard about my methods and wanted her mare started by me. She felt strongly that my nontraumatic approach would enhance the genuine qualities of the mustang, causing her to be an excellent riding animal for herself and her family.

This was the first mustang I had started since those early days of working with them in Salinas. I advised this lady that she should wait until the foal was six or seven months old and then wean it. Once the mare had settled down, she could bring her to the farm.

They duly arrived. The trailer was backed up to the round pen and out of it charged the wildest animal I have ever seen in my life. I soon learned that she had gone through the adoption program and had just been turned out in a corral. Her only interaction with humans was when they fed and watered her. It was a daunting experience to watch this mustang from the small viewing platform. She was frantically trying to climb out and kept herself as far away as possible from our side of the pen.

Eventually I entered the pen to begin to work with her. I went through my procedure, sending her away, which is the first step, and she responded quite well. She gave me the signs I was looking for and was very demonstrative. After about forty-five minutes I could touch her. We were making excellent progress. By the two-hour mark, I had a halter on her and was leading her around. I could pick up her front feet, but when I tried to pick up her back ones, she resisted furiously by kicking. Mustangs are often paranoid when it comes to handling their hind legs and I felt certain that a few days of work would increase her trust in me so that this problem would go away. I decided not to force that issue.

Sean, my assistant, brought in the saddle, bridle and pad, placing them in the center of the round pen. While he was doing this, the mare was hovering really close to me at the south side of the pen. Sean left to the north, closing the solid wooden gate behind him.

I left the south side of the pen and started to walk toward the equipment, leaving the mare just to the right of me. She was facing north toward the door. I took about two steps from the south wall and she left me like a rocket. Running as fast as she could, she crashed into the saddle on the ground and started ripping it to shreds with her teeth. Pawing and kicking, she tore at the saddle. It was as if I had brought a lion into the middle of the pen. I felt she thought she was cornered and had to fight this predator for her life. I stood frozen in my tracks near the south wall of the pen. The air was filled with bits and pieces as they flew off the saddle. The effect was terrifying and I must admit at that moment I thought I was next on the menu.

I started moving around to my right, staying as close as I could to the wall. I moved along as smoothly and rapidly as possible. I had recently had extensive back surgery, so jumping out of the round pen was not an option. I managed to get about halfway round. I saw Sean was standing on the viewing platform near the gate, watching me and at that moment the mare broke away from the saddle and ran straight at me.

My heart almost stopped. I was scared to death. I crouched down against the base of the wall and decided that the best way to take her on was to ball up in a fetal position covering my head. She was coming and having seen what she had done to the saddle, I knew it was not going to be pretty. I could sense that Sean had jumped down from his perch into the pen right by the gate. I don't think he was too anxious to get near her either, but the mere fact that he came into the pen said a lot for his courage.

As I was balled up there on the ground, I saw out of the corner of my eye her nose was right against the wall in front of me. She had not attacked me. Her hind feet were brushing against my toes. It was very strange because she was almost in a U shape, wrapping herself around me, her tail against the wall on one side and her nose the other.

I stayed balled up there for a while and Sean was out of sight. I saw her look over her shoulder directly at the saddle. As her head came off the wall to view the saddle she pinned her ears flat back and bared her teeth. As she looked back toward me her ears came forward and her mouth was closed. I called out to Sean. "Wait, wait, don't come forward now." Luckily she had not seen him as her attention was fixed on the saddle and me. He stopped in his tracks, frozen by my urgent command and stood up against the wall. The mare then made another dive for the saddle, attacking the remaining larger pieces. Like a whirlwind, she suddenly deserted this deadly enemy and resumed her protective stance around me.

I realized that this mare was adopting me. She had joined-up with me so intensely that in her mind I deserved the same protection as her foal. She was guarding me from this deadly predator that had come into our world. She was still lactating and the warm milk began to drip onto my legs.

Sean moved into the center of the pen and gathered up the shredded remnants that had been a saddle, retreated and closed the gate behind him. Once the potential danger was removed, the mare walked away from me. I got up, stroked her head and walked around the pen with her. Sean went for another saddle and returned to the pen. This time I kept her on a lead while putting the pad, saddle and bridle on.

Sean came in later and rode her with no trouble, finishing up in just over two and a half hours. The owner actually rode the mare within two weeks and was extremely pleased. Later reports reached me that this mare became a wonderful animal for both this lady and her daughter. It was the first mustang she had adopted and this experience was so positive that she became president of a mustang association.

Several times she invited me to come to adoption events and start mustangs, which I was delighted to do. She felt that they had a better chance of being successfully adopted if they were already "joined-up."

The bizarre behavior described in this story has never reoccurred with me, nor have I heard of it happening to anybody else. While the occurrence may have been unusual, her desire to protect me amplified the potential for close human-to-horse attachment. The mare's body language was there for me to read, but I was confused by the speed of events and perceived only the aggression with which she attacked the saddle. It took me a long time to realize that this was the act of a mother to protect what she now considered to be her family. I had not before realized the depth of bonding that Join-Up creates. In the mare's mind I was to be protected from all danger and that included a possible attack from what she perceived to be "the deadly saddle."

Surely one of the most important jobs a parent has to do is to protect the child from any kind of threat. This must be a deeply instinctual trait imbedded in the brains of all mammals. This mare exemplified the extent to which a mother will go to protect what she perceives to be her maternal responsibility.

A human being (predominantly a fight animal) will quite often act out in violence even when it is not in his best interest. I feel that most traditional horsemen would have stood their ground to this mare and wherever possible would have struck her, feeling it was the only way to protect themselves. Many of the horsemen I have known in my time would have literally beaten the hell out of her.

We all know now what a mistake an act of violence would have been at that moment in time. I believe that she would have instantly become a mare never again to trust a human under any circumstances.

We have been closely associated with the horse throughout almost the entire development of our species, and possibly this is why the concepts that I have explored in this book are as sound as they are.

This new millennium will be the first in the history of humankind without the horse as the mainstay of our transport system. The horse owes us nothing. They have fought with us in our wars, plowed our fields, fed us and remained the most faithful of servants. "Man's best friend" has probably been an accolade preserved for our dogs for a few thousand years now. I've heard it said the Egyptian pharaohs were the first to use this term. I love dogs and I believe that people can love them deeply and that dogs try to please us far more than most people will, but there is also a case for the horse being man's best friend.

The horse has been our partner in an incredible range of serious activities, and we must never forget the effort the horse has made to entertain us—racing, polo, dressage, jumping, rodeo and every kind of game or competition that you can imagine has been done in one form or another on horseback. The horse has served us as a pleasurable companion, to a greater degree than we realize. At the turn of the twentieth century the horse was our primary vehicle and practically the only power source on the farm. By the mid-1900s they were scarcely used in these ways, yet in the United States the total horse population at the turn of the twenty-first century was three times larger than it had been a hundred years before. How can this be when we don't need them anymore? Because we do need or want them for our entertainment and pleasure.

But there is more to Equus than just the enjoyment of all the sports and pastimes with which we associate the horse. We can use his natural existence as a metaphor for our lives today. I once believed it was nothing more than a metaphor, but I have discovered that the horse has many of the same responses and needs as humans; and the horse and human have closer behavioral ties than I had first considered. The reason horse and human work so well together may be because they do share much in common—the horse's behavior is not alien to us. It is little wonder that what the horses tell me in the language of Equus, their natural communication system, can be translated directly to the world of humans.

•

Recently, we had two very interesting horses brought to Flag Is Up Farms, which gave me a unique opportunity to test the true nature of this language. One was born without hearing and the other had been blind from birth. As events progressed the blind horse regained its sight following surgery, but the deaf horse will remain so for life. The deaf horse understood all my communication (in body language) and joined-up well with me. The once-blind horse had difficulty in deciphering my movements; they meant very little to it. These experiments proved that their body-language communication is to a great degree learned, although partly instinctual, and that sound is not terribly important. Mares might call to their foals or vice versa, and sounds will alert horses, but they do not play a major role in their communication system. "Actions speak louder than words" is a nice saying and one we humans use quite often; generally, however, we do not live by it. The language of Equus is, in fact, one of actions, not words.

If you still find it difficult to believe that sound is not a necessary element in the language of Equus, you only have to look at the behavior of a herd of wild horses. Every time I bring wild mustangs to the farm, they run and hide in horror at the neighing of domestic horses because they fear that a predator will be alerted. It is clear to me that this language I have identified is silent—it is a body language that utilizes direction, speed and gesture to receive and pass on information.

The most common forms of communication on earth are silent. Bioluminescence is used by billions of marine animals. It is a light show. Their little bodies are equipped with a lighting system that flashes in patterns only they understand. Body language is used by literally hundreds of species. It may seem to uninformed human beings that many gestures are without specific meaning, but be assured, the more you learn about body language, the more specific you find it to be.

Since 1986, when I first showed my work in public, thousands of people have come to Flag Is Up Farms from all industries and walks of life to watch me demonstrate Join-Up. Most of them had no idea what to expect. I noticed an odd phenomenon and began to make a mental note of its occurrence. At the beginning of a demonstration I send the horse away into flight mode around the pen, and when he shows that he is ready, I communicate an invitation to join me. The horse turns toward me, walks in close and reaches out to touch my shoulder with its nose. At this precise moment I often hear a gasp from the crowd. On several occasions I have actually heard the commotion as someone falls. After the person affected has recovered, he or she has relived with me stories of mental or physical abuse. Oftentimes women are reduced to tears at the sight of a flight animal accepting and trusting a potential predator. This is no coincidence: it happens too often.

The animal at the fight end of the fight/flight spectrum is a predator, and the animal at the flight end is preyed upon. Based on this assumption, you can describe humans as predators, but humans can also be passive, nonviolent and nonaggressive. This curious and perhaps unique mixture of fight and flight, prey and predator is almost always present in our relationships and communications. Women, in particular, have a great ability to identify with the hunted and therefore with horses.

The traditional horse trainer who breaks a horse by tying him up and forcing him to accept saddle, bridle and rider is a predator. Male predatorial behavior is far more common than most people would imagine, and it happens in our apparently enlightened society on a scale that I find difficult to comprehend. In many parts of the world, women are still expected to walk behind their husbands and have few or no rights. Women in and out of the workplace are often preyed upon. It is little wonder that women identify with the flight animal.

The thousands of letters sent to me tell a sad story of the continuing existence of abuse of all kinds, predominantly in the home. How long will it take to raise awareness that violence is never the answer?

If the similarities between human and horse can tell us anything, it is this: the horse has much to teach us about social structure. He is asking not to be preyed upon. He is begging to Join-Up, to become a member of the human herd, a fifty-fifty partner on the basis of trust, and for us to leave violence out of the contract. Many women who watch my work will remark that they wish this lesson could be learned by the male of our species. When a man learns that a nonviolent approach can be far more effective—

for himself as well as the prey animal—he understands how wrong violence is.

While I have learned the value of a good academic education, no hands-on work can be totally replaced by theory. It's also true that at the time of my university training, there were no courses that approximated the work that I do. My teachers were a few people and many thousands of horses. I spent long hours with a pair of binoculars watching and learning about the nature, behavior and language of horses. I observed in detail and gradually translated it into a system that, coupled with my love for horses, formed the foundation for Join-Up. I am still learning, still discovering and still refining my approach.

It is my hope that Join-Up will one day be accepted as truly revolutionary in both the horse and human worlds. In my work, as in the work of other horse gentlers, the horse is given the opportunity to make choices, and to volunteer to cooperate with humans. It is my deepest wish that this discovery helps to change the nature of human interactions.

What is, I believe, unique in my approach is that I have recognized in the horse a language of communication from which we, as humans, can learn fundamentally important lessons. The last six thousand horses of the more than ten thousand I have started (that is, convinced them to willingly accept saddle, bridle and rider) averaged under thirty minutes to accomplish the goals described here. It is no great feat for me, and I should not be credited with inventing anything. I have only discovered what nature already had in place, a language and an understanding of how two species can get along without violence.

HOW TO ACHIEVE JOIN-UP

To understand the important principles behind Join-Up and how we can transfer them to our world, I will quickly take you through the process of Join-Up itself.

The horse has a very effective and discernible language. The incredible thing about this language is that it is universal to the species. Humans, on the other hand, possessing the most phenomenal brains on earth, often need help to communicate with one another. Just like any other form of communication, the language of Equus requires some effort to master. If we refuse to believe that the horse can communicate fluently, then we are apt to fall into the trap of training through the use of pain. Consider for a moment what you would feel if, when you attended your first day of school, your teacher put a chain through your mouth or over your nose, gave it a jerk and then took a whip to you when you tried to get away. What do you believe the balance of your relationship would have been? How do you think you would have viewed school from that point on?

Although horses' brains are not as complex as humans', horses have a similar reaction. The point of my method is to create a relationship based on trust and confidence, a relationship by which the horse wants to Join-Up, be part of the team and wear the same color jersey. Most conventionally broken horses form an adversarial relationship with the people they work for and, though they may agree to perform, it is with reluctance. Any environment that is based on fear and punishment will achieve performance, but not innovation. You can force people and horses to cooperate, but you cannot force optimum performance. This desire to perform can only be achieved through intrinsic motivation.

When starting the fresh horse I will not hit, kick, jerk, pull or tie to restrain him. I request that he perform certain maneuvers, but I must not force or demand. The horse is the quintessential flight animal and when any pressure is applied to the relationship, he will almost always choose to leave rather than fight. I have chosen to follow a nonconfrontational route, and my intention is to cause the animal to accept the saddle, bridle and rider with a minimum of trauma. I regularly do public demonstrations where I take a young horse who has not been saddled, bridled or ridden and attempt to have him accept all this in approximately thirty minutes.

I bring the horse into my round pen where I introduce myself in the center of the circle. After this brief get-acquainted session, I offer the horse an opportunity to leave me. I square up to the animal and snap my eyes directly on to his—what I call "eyes on eyes." The horse, viewing this as a predatory gesture, flees. I track the horse as he proceeds around the perimeter of the pen so that my shoulders are square with him at all times. My eyes pierce his. In his language this means, "Go away."

My message to him is, "You made the choice to go away and that is fine, but don't go away a little, go away a lot." Horses have a flight distance of approximately a quarter to three-eighths of a mile. After that, they feel compelled to negotiate with their predator, as it could be dangerous to continue fleeing because they run out of energy. Once this distance has been achieved, their tendency is to request a truce of some sort.

I remain eyes on eyes and shoulders square, but I watch closely for gestures of negotiation—gestures that make up part of the language of Equus that I've deciphered over time. The first one I virtually always see is that he will lock on me the ear closest to me. It will point in my direction. This means, "I respect you. I don't know who you are or what you are up to, but I will show you respect and attempt a negotiation." Second, he will come off the wall and try to come closer to me, near the middle of the pen. I remain shoulders square, eyes on eyes, which effectively keeps him away. The next gesture I usually observe is that he licks and chews—language, in effect, that conveys he does not fear me and believes I will not hurt him. The fourth and last gesture that I wait to receive is when the horse drops his head down near the soil and allows it to bounce along. This says, "If we could have a meeting to renegotiate, I would let you be the chairman."

With all four of these gestures in place, I take my eyes away from his eyes, turn slightly away from him and set my shoulders on a forty-five degree angle to the body axis of the horse. This means that he is entitled to come to me, to make a choice to be with me rather than to go away. I stand virtually motionless as he approaches and reaches his nose out, most often nudging me in the back. This is the moment of Join-Up, when the horse has chosen to accept me.

I turn slowly, eyes cast down between his front legs, my shoulders round, fingers closed and wrist bent. I reach up and rub him between the eyes. This is his reward for joining with me. Very occasionally the horse is not ready for Join-Up and returns to the flight mode and I have to repeat the process. Usually, however, after a few seconds of rubbing, I walk away and the horse will follow me. I call this Follow-Up. I can literally walk a serpentine pattern in the round pen and the horse is happy to follow close to my shoulder. I stop and turn slowly to stroke him once again, reaffirming our new relationship. Soon we will be partners doing great things.

If all learning is 0–10, then the most important part of learning is 0–1. Join-Up and Follow-Up represent the 0–1 phase. Once I have my horse traveling on a positive path, then all I have to do is reward him for his positive actions and put him to work if he does something negative. For the horse, work is running away from a predator. (The horse is at rest when he is peacefully grazing and must flee when danger is near in order to survive. However, it's also important to note that in order for the horse to maintain fitness he plays and runs with others.)

Once the horse is on that positive path, the balance of the procedure is academic. Before I ask him to accept certain responsibilities, I must earn his trust by showing him I am not a predator. To that end, we work our way through a series of goals. One is to massage with both hands those areas most often attacked by predators—high on the back and low into the soft flanks. I stroke the horse and then walk away, so that he becomes aware that I have no agenda to cause him pain. I pick up and put down each of his feet, then once more walk away to achieve the same result. After that come the saddle pad, saddle, bridle and rider.

If he says no to the saddle, he goes back to work, which means I gently but firmly push him away from me and require him to run around the perimeter of the round pen once more. The same goes for the bit and the other goals I choose for the horse. Often, placing the bit in his mouth causes the horse to forget about the saddle and think about this new item of tack—it causes a diversion. (Such a diversionary tactic can, we all know, be useful in dealing with reluctant children. If they are focused on a negative problem, then diverting their attention to something else is often a swift and effective way of turning a negative situation into a positive one.)

At no time is there a need to inflict pain or use violence. It will only cause the horse to want to fight me and is, without any question, counterproductive.

At this point, I have essentially accomplished my aim to have the horse accept the saddle, bridle and rider. The horse is not traumatized and elects to stay with me. And to my mind, this is the secret of true leadership. An effective leader must create a situation whereby people choose to stay with him or her rather than go away.

•

There are clear parallels between the procedure I describe above and certain aspects of human communication. With horses the methods are physical; with humans they are psychological. But they are both rooted in psychology and the results are the same phenomenon of acceptance, which will be predictable, discernible and effective.

First impressions are perhaps the most important messages we convey. There is never a second chance to make a first impression and the importance of the manner of a greeting can never be overstated. We humans can tell much from a handshake. Does it have a feeling of welcome and warmth or the lack of it? Rubbing the horse on the forehead I believe to be quite similar to the human handshake. People seem to be most comfortable after a handshake when they remain eye to eye and begin to communicate. Horses, on the other hand, do not require eye contact in this situation and are happiest when the human walks away from them immediately after rubbing the forehead. The horse will generally follow the human being at this point. Predators do not ordinarily walk away from prey animals. When I rub the forehead of my equine student and then walk away from him I am conveying the message that I am not acting predatorily. Touch and connection are established, however briefly, at this point. This welcome gives confidence to each party about the other's intentions. An embrace, too, can be such a reward. A hug is a wonderful reward for friendship given and establishes its continuance.

Eyes on eyes, shoulders square and encouraging the horse to go away is the same as allowing people to consider their options and recognize their mutual needs. Generally eye-to-eye contact between people implies communication is going to follow.

It can, however, also be a hostile gesture. The piercing eye-to-eye contact of the predator and prey is aggressive and implies intent to attack. A man was in a canteen one day, his lunch on his tray, when he was suddenly punched in the eye by a complete stranger. The man next to him was horrified and offered a helping hand. As they sat down together the man who had been attacked tried to piece together the reason for the assault. He told his new-found friend that the stranger caught his eye because he looked exactly like the man who had robbed him in the street just a week earlier. "I must have looked at him with subconscious aggression in my eyes without realizing it," he said thoughtfully.

My eye-to-eye contact with the horse communicates my desire for the animal to go away. I establish a working alliance and a flow of conversation only after the horse communicates a request for cooperation. Using the language of Equus, I keep the conversation alive as I create an environment for learning. If I execute true to the concepts of Join-Up I will soon establish trust. Ambivalence should not be viewed as resistance, but as a request for time to think over the proposal currently being offered. At no time should the trainer use force to establish leadership to achieve his or her aims.

When the horse turns his nearest ear toward me he is paying close attention to what I am saying. It is his first offering of respect during this act of communication.

Coming closer to me in the center of the circle is the equivalent of a person watching me closely during a conversation, and appearing to be keenly aware of what I am saying.

Licking and chewing, another part of the wordless conversation between horse and man, also has a broad connection to human communication. When the horse is still suckling from his mother, he moves his mouth in a unique manner, quite similar to the movements of a human baby. Once the horse has learned to eat grass and hay, this changes to a licking and chewing motion. Don't we humans place great importance on sharing a meal with someone with whom we wish to communicate? There is a great deal of meaning in this. "Let's have lunch together," is very different from, "Let's spend thirty minutes in my office." Going out to dinner is another level altogether. It metaphorically shows your soft underside and builds an environment of trust. After my first meeting with Queen Elizabeth many people asked me if I had dined with her. It was surprising to me at the time, but it made me acutely aware of how important most people feel it is to have shared a meal with someone. There is a subconscious understanding that sharing food suggests a closer association. Horses understand their own vulnerability while eating, and so that activity is reserved for a time when they are in the presence of those they trust.

When the horse drops his head and trots along bouncing it near the soil, he is acting out a very similar gesture to that of bowing in traditional Japanese culture: the person who achieves the lower position in this gesture of greeting is in fact asking the other to lead the conversation. This is virtually a direct translation of what the horse is saying: "Please suggest the agenda for this meeting. I don't necessarily want to be subservient to you, but one of us has to play the lead role and I would like it to be you."

The Join-Up moment is what any successful human conversation tries to achieve. It represents the coming together of two people, a meeting of the minds and of mutual respect and understanding. It advances the thought that I am happy to be with you and that I hope our time together will be one of mutual enjoyment. I place enormous importance on the fact that it is volunteered. With people, as with horses, I believe it is vital to achieve that same feeling of Join-Up. It is not possible to Join-Up when either participant feels pressure to accomplish it. It is not that we agreed to do it; it is that we want to do it.

Follow-Up is when I walk away from the horse after Join-Up. He will follow me only if he has a true desire to be with me. Horses have no ability to contrive. They simply cannot fake it. When I walk away, if he has any reticence about being with me, he certainly will not follow. Isn't this similar to forming a close association with another person, nurturing that association and then waiting to see if your new friend makes any effort to come to

you? If none is made, perhaps you need a bit more time to convince this individual that you have a meaningful role to play in his
or her life. In my opinion, this is the same whether in business or
personal relationships.

At the conclusion of a Join-Up session with a horse I make a
point of doing something that is generally fun for both my audience and me. I take my horse to one side of the round pen, then
run to the opposite side and ask my audience to applaud for the
horse's performance. The horse will virtually always perceive
noise as frightening and will rush to be close to me. The crowd
will at once realize that my horse has learned to seek a position
near me when danger is perceived, thus validating my concepts.

I mentioned that during each of my Join-Up procedures I
stroke the horse with both hands in what I call his vulnerable
areas, those spots most often attacked by predators, then walk
away. I do this to convince the horse that I intend him no harm.
No predator walks away from its prey once it has access to the
vulnerable areas. This builds trust. People are much the same, and
while vulnerability may be either physical or psychological, you
build trust when you are in a position where you could do harm
but you don't: the same is true when you protect another person
from something you believe could be harmful. In turn, you know
that if the same is done for you, it will increase your level of trust
for the person involved. This gesture confirms the trust that began to develop at the first greeting. This trust-building tool is one
of the most powerful in the world of commerce—the sharing of
personal experiences between colleagues helps to create an environment in which people can work at a closer and more efficient
level.

To further build this trust, I pick up each of the horse's
feet, hold it for a few seconds, put it down and walk away. The
horses' legs and feet are virtually their only weapons against predators. Their first choice is to flee using those powerful legs, but

they will fight as a last resort. The strike of a front hoof or the kick of a back one can often mean life for the horse instead of death. When a horse chooses to allow me control of his hooves, he is in fact entrusting me with his weapons. Isn't it true in the human spectrum that before we can go forward in a trust-based relationship, we are obligated to lay down our weapons? It isn't until both parties feel no need for armament that we can truly work in unison.

The saddle pad corresponds in human terms to a tentative step toward shouldering first responsibility. The question asked of us might be: "Are you going to be responsible for your own decisions?" It is useful to find out how people will react to the idea of responsibility before it is given. For example: engagement before marriage, internship before becoming a practitioner and apprenticeship before achieving professional status.

The saddle continues the testing and accepting. It is literally about carrying responsibility; "being saddled with" describes the assignment of a task. Acceptance of the saddle is a metaphor for facing up to responsibility and accepting the responsibility of further challenges.

The bridle is used to guide the horse. Taking the bit between the teeth means, in human terms, to put energy into something, to be purposeful. The bridle is used for gentle guidance, not to control. If a horse wanted to do something, a bridle would not stop him. Among people, guidance—or the willing acceptance of guidance—suggests that a trust mechanism is in place and that one person is listening to another. The bridle represents purpose and direction based upon communication and trust. Cohesive direction and good communication create teamwork, which we rely upon to achieve shared goals.

The rider is the ultimate responsibility for the horse—a commitment akin to that of a partnership or marriage. The partnership of horse and rider represents the mutual acceptance of responsibility between employer and employee, teacher and student, husband and wife. Trust between horse and human can be seen when the two partners are relaxed and at peace together, where there is no force or stress involved.

It cannot be overemphasized that any violence will undo the processes I've just described above.

JOIN-UP: THE JOURNEY

Join-Up is a tool, like a fine chisel. With it, you can carve a stable environment that enables communication. The tool must be used with skill, which may take years to perfect, but in its basic form Join-Up can be learned quickly.

It is, though, a procedure that must be precisely followed; there are no shortcuts. Each step is distinct and necessary. Join-Up may bring out conflict and perceived resistance or ambivalence. It is imperative that anyone using Join-Up be totally responsible for his own actions while allowing the other party to be responsible for his.

A raw horse that quickly accepts saddle, bridle and rider does so, in part, because he has been offered freedom of choice. The "trainer" simply moves through the process, keeping the conversation alive, always allowing the horse time to respond.

It is therefore *response*-based, not *demand*-based. You have to learn to open the doors of opportunity and be confident that Join-Up will work. You may have to wait until the horse responds favorably—the same holds true in human relationships.

Join-Up works at any stage of a relationship, whether a new one or one of long standing. It heralds an end to isolation by establishing bonding through communication. Join-Up is the result of deep communication in a shared language; it is a bond based on trust and marks the beginning of a fifty-fifty partnership, sustained through continued adherence to Join-Up's principles and techniques. It is nonviolent, noncoercive and can only be achieved if both partners have willingly entered into the process. Join-Up means stepping into the other person's world, by observing his or her needs, conditions, rules and by working within *his* framework and communicating in *his* language. It is not created by a particular environment, nor is it a formula to overcome an inability to communicate. It cannot be faked.

On the other hand, it can be formulated and taught; at heart it's a simple process. Once you understand the formula, the path is clear to successful and mutually enjoyable conversation.

Follow-Up is the confirmation of Join-Up. With horses, this process allows the trainer to reestablish the trust bond. If the bond is not firm enough, the trainer simply goes back through the process until Join-Up is reestablished. Join-Up's strength is its simplicity.

Join-Up is pivotal to a balanced existence, encouraging trust, reliability and comfort from others, but it can only occur when an underlying desire for partnership exists on both sides. My training provides a step-by-step guide to building a trust-based partnership, which is essential for horses and humans in order to eliminate violence.

With humans, as with horses, communication enables Join-Up. Trust keeps the process alive.

JOIN-UP IN THE WORKPLACE

Fear and mistrust can be delivered to you by two distinctly different messengers. First "the familiar" and second "the unfamiliar." Horses bring about fear in people, generally because they are unfamiliar with them. People simply have not taken the time to get to know that, although horses are large and fast, they have no agenda to hurt without cause. Fear of a parent, your spouse or your boss might be established out of familiarity and a knowledge that they have a propensity to "act out" violently.

I tell people who express great fear of horses to get to know them, to study their true patterns of behavior and understand more clearly what the horse wants out of life before branding them as dangerous.

As I examine my own patterns of fear and distrust, it seems utterly foreign to think that I might fear a horse. It is a joke for me to think that I might fear this flight animal more than the man walking on the other side of the street or the person approaching in an automobile. It seems ridiculous to me that a horse could be perceived as more dangerous than an airplane, train, truck or even that awesome instrument of terror, the computer.

What the horses are telling me is that if you can remove fear from the environment, both learning and innovation spiral upward. There is no more fearful situation than when people in the workplace are faced with change. Predictability and routine are all important in the stress-filled world of business. If you take away that predictability, change the routine, you alter the environment in which people work. Change, however, is with us. The speed of change in today's high-tech world is frightening. One of the most important jobs a manager has is to create an environment in which change occurs without production loss. This can be accomplished by creating an environment in which people are willing to change. Obtaining people's willingness to embrace change is therefore a catalyst in the process of change.

I ask my raw horse to change from being an uncooperative animal to being a partner with me in a new venture. I do not use force—horses Join-Up with me of their own free will. It should be the same with a workforce. Without willingness, work suffers and the whole organization is crippled. Take the simple situation of lunch and coffee breaks, time off and bonus benefits. If a manager is fearful that the company's goodwill is being abused, he may try to control the situation forcefully. What he should do is concentrate on making the working environment pleasant and building motivation so that the employee is actually happy to stay busy. If the executive gets his formula right, he may well find that his attention will need to be directed to seeing to it that his people take sufficient time off so as to freshen them for the task. Suddenly you have employees hungry to volunteer their loyalty, in the same way that horses lick and chew to signal their willingness to cooperate. People, like horses, perform much better if they are willing partners.

While attending a conference I noticed that one company put its management team in one hotel and its executives in another more upscale establishment. If cooperation and communication are desirable, then segregation is destructive. In my own organization, I attempt at all times to keep travel and living accommodation the same for all staff to promote the feeling of being a member of the team. I work to create an environment that communicates this theme: each position on the team is important if we are to achieve a successful outcome on tour and at our demonstrations.

On another occasion, a well-known organization came to Flag Is Up Farms for a demonstration. The employees filed up onto the round pen viewing platform. Three of the executives stood by the buses—I was told they were the bosses and we would have to wait for them before I could start. I took no notice and began my introduction. I didn't see why 98 percent of the people should have to wait for the 2 percent. As the crowd hushed and the sound system came on, I could see the three men had come up the steps and were standing to the rear of the onlookers. In an oblique way I began to describe how corporate families find ways to intimidate and pull rank on their workforce. I didn't name the men, but I made my position clear to everyone.

Remaining on the theme throughout the evening worked like a charm and, at the end, each of those men came to me and told me how much they had learned that night.

A CORPORATE EXPERIENCE

Paradyne

Paradyne employs more than 800 people at its corporate headquarters in the Tampa Bay area of Florida in the United States and has regional offices around the world. Paradyne is a pioneer in high-speed network access and is revolutionizing the data communications industry. More than 50 percent of Fortune 500 companies, and businesses in more than 125 countries, have chosen Paradyne.

In 1997, Paradyne had a huge challenge on its hands. The company needed to adopt a new information management system, and get it up and working in eighteen months or less. The company had an archaic information system. It was necessary to install a new system, which would change everything they were doing, from giving a quote to organizing payment at the other end. John Guest of Paradyne brought in management consultants. They put together a team of people in charge of getting change under way and titled it "the foundation team." The consultants showed the foundation team my Join-Up video. They were not at all sure how the film would be accepted—after all, I was a cowboy talking about horses.

The consultants needed to stir up creativity and willingness, and began by exposing the team to metaphors from the horse world. Time was limited: they had only two days to put the team together. To take an hour out of those critical days to see a video about a horseman was a bold step for these consultants. Would the foundation team see the connection between the nonconfrontational methods I use with horses and its need for people to accept a completely new information system? The team was asked to write down all the connections they saw between the project in front of them and the film. Within two minutes people were nodding, then busy writing and listing the connections as they saw them—more than a hundred in all, including: a nontraumatic, noncoercive environment; allowing bucking to occur; expecting resistance; keeping the pulse rate down; establishing trust; and keeping the dialogue flowing. They recognized the value of never taking out their frustrations on a colleague.

The consultant team sat back at this point, breathed a deep sigh of relief and realized the message was getting through. Join-Up became a metaphor for the willing acceptance of change that the team sought.

The film helped to establish the tone of the workshops and the changeover to the new system went well. In record time, Paradyne was reaping the benefits of change, with a level of acceptance its executives had previously not considered possible.

In 1999, I was in Texas meeting with my friend Flip Flippen about his work with the school systems in parts of that state. And as an aid to our conversation he told me about an interesting experience he had with Transit Mix.

A CORPORATE EXPERIENCE

Transit Mix

Join-Up has the power to transform a workplace in terms of efficiency and employees' motivation and satisfaction. Turns out Transit Mix Concrete & Material Corporation was in real need of all three.

It faced mounting costs caused by high turnover among the

drivers of trucks used to deliver concrete and materials. It was cost-
ing the firm $2,200 to train a driver and the turnover rate was a
staggering 72 percent every six months. The cost of accidents also
cut deeply into its profits.

Flip Flippen of M. B. Flippen Associates was brought in by
Mark Stiles, president of Transit Mix, to meet company executives
and improve performance. Flip is a psychotherapist who owns one
of the most successful teacher-educator companies in America. In
1997 he was lying in bed reading alongside his wife, Susan, who
was watching a PBS special, a documentary on my gentling of the
wild mustang Shy Boy in the high desert. Half listening, at first he
thought the program was about kids, not horses, but he soon sat up
and listened attentively to the rest of the documentary.

Later, he bought a copy of the video and asked some of his staff
to watch it. They were fascinated but didn't get its relevance to
their work until Flip asked them to close their eyes and listen. "Tell
me," he asked. "Is he talking about horses or kids?"

Flip became a close friend and we later collaborated on a video
used for instructional purposes in the school system. Although I
had developed my approach from my work with horses and his had
grown from his knowledge of children and teachers, there was a
strong relationship between my concepts and his teaching methods. Although his work is primarily educating teachers who work
with children, he and I had been collaborating for about a year
when he got the call from Transit Mix, which asked him if he could
use his renowned skills for improving educational performance to
help solve its corporate problems. Flip took a hard look at the
driver problem. Cement trucks carry a heavy load that rides high
over the truck's mainframe. With that high center of gravity, these
vehicles are prone to overturn at the slightest miscue. The drivers
are in charge of loading and unloading, washing the truck after
each off-loading and preparing their unit for the next trip. The
work is strenuous and the scheduling tension-packed. And when

drivers quit, qualified replacements were scarce—in part due to a construction boom and an all-time low unemployment rate in Texas.

Another area of concern was property damage. Because of high turnover, competent operation of the vehicles was at a low level. Backing into someone's building or crunching the contractor's Mercedes was an expensive proposition.

After a few days of observation, Flip had identified what he believed was the primary problem. "The company and these drivers," he said, "have not joined-up. I found a window, up high in the office building where I could see a large portion of the operation. I watched the drivers arriving in the morning, parking their cars, taking over their trucks and starting their day. They never talked to anybody and no one spoke to them. When their truck was loaded, off they went, getting directions from a dispatcher on their CB radios."

Flip concluded that the drivers were seen as little more than robots. When he met them to hear their concerns, he discovered that they were completely disengaged from the company. Their basic concern was "When is pay day and how much do I get?"

Flip and I had discussed the fact that every time I do Join-Up with a horse, I give him a rub between the eyes; I let him know that I care; then I communicate with him, form a relationship and earn his trust and respect. Flip then put in place the EXCEL Leadership Model, which he uses with teachers. It consists of a series of steps almost identical to my own in the round pen. As in Join-Up, first comes the welcome—one of the most important phases of building trust. My rubbing of the horse's forehead is analogous to offering a handshake, saying "hello" and exchanging pleasantries. Flip told Transit Mix executives that they had to listen to the needs of their employees, much as I listen to my horses.

Flip spent considerable time with the executives and established their individual needs and wishes, both for their working lives and for the company—he literally joined-up with them and urged them to *engage* with their drivers in the same fashion. He went around the room shaking their hands, asking them if they had ever shaken the hands of their drivers. Each had to admit that he had not, and all agreed to give the plan their best shot. This was vital, because it is impossible to make significant change in a company unless you have agreement at the top level.

The executives had to convey concern, interest and commitment to the truck drivers and let them know that they were important and respected employees. They started meeting the drivers every morning, shaking their hands and exchanging a few words about their plans for the day. A new company attitude began to take shape.

New drivers and their families, many of whom spoke Spanish as their first language, experienced difficulties when first coming to town. So the company hired a social worker to help relocating families with telephone or electrical hookups, in registering children in school or finding a doctor. The social worker even went to workers' homes to discuss with spouses things such as job benefits and preschool classes, how to find tutoring services or set up car pools, since the head of the household often drove the family's only vehicle to work. Taking a lot of the stress out of matters at home left the men better able to concentrate on work. The social worker's job was equivalent to Follow-Up, which enables the trainer to create a bond of trust with the horse. The workers had found a safe place, which enabled them to respect their managers and give their commitment to the partnership.

At one point, the child of a driver became seriously ill. The company helped out and it was astonishing how many other drivers showed up to help the family as well. Transit Mix suddenly had a team.

Flip then decided to bring company executives to watch one of my demonstrations where they too learned the power of Join-Up.

Managers went back to work with a new enthusiasm, which they communicated to employees, and goodwill flourished. Shop mechanics would shake hands with drivers; there was a new willingness to work harder to resolve problems.

At the same time Transit Mix executives, Bill McWhirter, president, and Haywood Walker, COO, under Flip's guidance, instituted a certified professional driver program. After a thorough training course, certified drivers got a bonus, a raise and a patch for their uniforms. This created an elite corps within the drivers' group. Men who were proud to do a good job were rewarded for their efforts.

Competition for the certification courses encouraged drivers to stay with Transit Mix. There were even competitions between plants to select the most outstanding driver. The company discovered the value of giving positive rewards for positive actions. Employees' efforts were rewarded with care and commitment. To anyone who has watched me work with a horse in a round pen, it all sounds familiar.

Most of the drivers came to the company with lots of baggage. They had spent their lives relegated to low-paying jobs and they were not used to being treated with respect. At first they were skeptical; they were unaccustomed to a handshake from the bosses, but it wasn't long before they saw the workplace as a safe place and their effort increased dramatically.

Mark Stiles, group president, set the tone and direction for a successful future. The driver turnover rate dropped from 72 percent to 47 percent in just over fourteen months. The dropout rate among certified drivers was less than 1 percent. Transit Mix is confident that the dropout rate will continue to fall sharply. Meanwhile, the company now serves as a model for the trucking industry, and Transit Mix is more profitable than ever.

Two

COMMUNICATION

*The body language of horses offers
profound lessons for communication
between humans.*

Communication is key to our success as human beings. Poor communication results in unrest, unhappiness, isolation and much more. The horse communicates through body language. With humans, body language plays an important role in determining what information we receive and how we are receiving it. Surprisingly, words play a relatively insignificant role in our interaction with people. Therefore nonverbal communication sends very strong messages, not only in the world of the equine and most other animal species, but also among humans.

If we feel comfortable around someone, we will naturally want to stay with him. By staying near him, we are likely to become more interested in him, his needs and desires. This is how we influence people.* Scientific evidence allows us to assume that

*Intuition tells us, and research confirms this, that nonverbal communication is a major force in our lives. In fact, it has been estimated that

about 80 percent of communication between humans is body language. When compared with words, body language cues are imprinted more deeply in the human memory bank. Tone of voice is the next most influential part of communication and words make up the rest. This compares favorably with the horse's communication system. Horses communicate extensively and almost entirely using body language: they do make noises, but in the natural environment, silence is paramount, because no member of the herd wants to alert predators. The horse's highly developed senses of smell and eyesight play an important part in their communication.

The dictionary definition of communication is an act or instance of transmitting information. But communication is so much more than that. What are we trying to do when we communicate with people? We are looking for *physical, emotional and spiritual families.* We are looking for like-minded people who will reduce our sense of isolation in an increasingly complex world. The horse knows that, in his world, isolation means certain death. People, by contrast, can often intentionally isolate themselves from other humans. Though they can survive quite well, isolation can have negative consequences. In large cities for example, fear for one's safety tends to create a desire to isolate oneself using bigger and bigger locks and more and more security, creating an en-

---

nearly two-thirds of the meaning in any social situation is derived from nonverbal cues (Birdwhistell, 1955). A more extreme estimate touted in the popular literature is that 93 percent of all meaning is nonverbal (Mehrabian & Ferris, 1967). This estimate is an overestimate, however (as discussed in chapter 5). Regardless of the actual percentage of meaning that can be attributed to nonverbal cues, there is abundant evidence that people rely heavily on nonverbal cues to express themselves and to interpret the communicative activity of others. (Judee K. Burgoon, David B. Buller and W. Gill Woodall, *Nonverbal Communication: The Unspoken Dialogue*, New York: McGraw-Hill, 1996.)

vironment of isolation within the mass of humanity. And often people in isolation lose confidence both socially and in the workplace. Stress and loneliness rise and isolation can create a sense of vulnerability.

The badly behaved foal that has been sent out of the herd knows that he cannot survive alone without the protection provided by the group. The isolated horse is at risk. The elderly or infirm horse unable to sustain the pace of the family lags behind and is soon harvested by predators. The horse knows that isolation is an unhealthy state, whereas the human seems to be unaware of the potential dangers of solitary confinement, even when it's by choice.

Animals use a sophisticated interspecies communication system in order to survive. They assist each other, protect and communicate in a way man has yet to learn. Animals do not form subversive groups that terrorize the neighborhood as humans have learned to do. To be isolated is not to be part of a community, not to belong. Isolation is a revolt against all the things society has to offer. The more people find themselves in situations where isolation is encouraged, accepted and endured, the more anger, shame and fear they will feel. And reactions such as violent crime will surely be a result. We need to improve our communication with the less fortunate of our society and learn to speak the language they understand, as I have with the horse.

When I induce the horse to circle the round pen I am saying, "I am giving you an opportunity to choose for yourself. Flee if that is what you feel is best for you." I want the horse to be free to choose his own course because in that state of mind learning is encouraged. Through communication, I play out the role of predator and await the gestures appropriate to renegotiation. When the horse exercises his option to come to me rather than go away, I welcome him as strongly as I can in the language of Equus. I reinforce his choice so that we can work together in harmony. It is my hope that we can go forward from that point in the certain knowledge that we mean no harm to one another.

FATHER AND SON

It's important to realize that we do each other harm in many ways—physical violence is only one form of violence. Harm can be done verbally or by an absence of communication. Communication, and the lack of it, molds our personalities just as the sculptor's hands mold clay. If we find a way to come together with others, each of us understanding our mutual needs and desires, a bond forms. True communication protects us from misunderstandings that tend to fester into a state of fear and distrust. To acquire trust in a relationship is one of the most enriching aspects of life. But my own life is testament to the fact that communication between humans—even between father and son—is often flawed or lacking altogether.

I was walking down Main Street in our hometown of Salinas one day; I would guess I was about ten at the time. I looked ahead and saw my father walking directly toward me. As he approached, I said, "Hi Dad!" but he looked at me and kept walking. I couldn't decide if he had seen me or not so I said, "Dad . . . Hello!" He was only about three feet from me and he looked directly at me. I could tell that he recognized me, that he knew me, but he gave no response at all. He passed me, turned to the left, and crossed the street; again I called out to him, "Dad. Hey!" I shouted loud enough for the whole neighborhood to hear, but he just kept walking. I returned to school, hurt and puzzled, trying to figure out in my mind what I could have done to upset him and cause him to so deliberately ignore me.

I harbored this hurt for many years. My father's recognition of me was important, particularly at that age. This incident was yet another deep scar on our relationship. In a sense, it was a small incident, but it reflected a huge coldness, a void between us, which I simply could never come to grips with. I became always eager to please. I did everything he wanted me to. I intensely disliked being involved in his harsh, often brutal if traditional training methods with horses, but in order to please him I gave him any assistance he requested.

We finally reached a silent understanding. During a confrontation years later, I asked him if he remembered that day on the street when he ignored me. He looked at me and said, "I didn't have anything to say to you." I let it go, because I guess that was an answer; by then I knew it would achieve nothing to point out that I had not been asking for a conversation that day in Salinas, merely an acknowledgment of my presence.

Greetings take little effort. Children need to know they are important to someone. A parent refusing to acknowledge the presence of his child is like an animal refusing to allow a newborn to drink from its udder. It is a refusal of life itself. I have been strong in my need to communicate with my own children because of such incidents from my childhood. Parents must take responsibility for their children's emotional welfare; the impressions of humanity they grow up with will mold their lives and affect the lives of the people around them.

For a few critical years in my development I lived with the knowledge that my father had ignored me. The child will almost always ask, Why? In this case the child's logical conclusion was that he wasn't worthy of a greeting. A child so treated will often conclude that he or she has been rejected by society, in this first case the microsociety of his immediate family. If a message of rejection is given to a child, we should not be surprised if the child rejects the family and, perhaps, in the end, the larger society. We have already painted the picture; all the child has to do is step into it.

I had not, to the best of my knowledge, done anything to cause my father to ignore me. In my own opinion, I was a hard-working youngster whom any father might have been proud to have raised. The incident, however, caused doubt in me, and it left an indelible mark on my character that has caused me to view relationships with people with a degree of skepticism. But if the adults in my life didn't seem to make much sense, the horses—even, and especially, wild horses—were starting to make perfect sense.

DISCOVERING THE LANGUAGE OF EQUUS

In 1948 I made my first of many trips to Nevada. There, deep in the heart of Indian and ranching country, I watched the wild mustangs and began to recognize that there was a decipherable vocabulary in their actions and movements. There were quiet times during our trek in which I could observe the mustangs interacting with one another oblivious to our presence. I was driven more by intuition than by a desire to communicate with horses, but this experience opened the door to a process of communication that would help me find common ground between human and horse.

Advance and retreat was one of the first lessons taught to me by horses and I was later to discover that it works well with people, too! This was an exciting time for me as I was discovering the presence of a language that nature probably had had in place for millions of years.

This early knowledge was the foundation of all that I am today as a horseman. A few years later, as a boy of fifteen, I was convinced that it would be possible to get a wild mustang to turn and come back to me of his own volition, so that he would Join-Up with me instead of fleeing. It was a wild undertaking, but out there in the desert in 1951, I caused a mustang colt, about three or four years old, to Join-Up with me in one day.

I started out early one morning and within a couple of hours or so I had a young mustang separated from the herd and was driving him away from the group by using what I now know to be crude gestures in the language of Equus. Even though I had a lot to learn I was able to utilize the principles of advance and retreat to make it uncomfortable for him when he was negative and very comfortable for him when he was positive. Within twenty-four hours, having stopped to feed and water my saddle horses while allowing the mustang to do the same, I had full control over the movements of this wild flight animal. I could square up on him with my saddle horse and run straight at him if he decided to leave me. I would stop abruptly, turning to ride away if he showed me the signs that he wanted to come closer to me. In one full day I could cause him to willingly follow me around. His actions became voluntary. He was relaxed and comfortable. I didn't take it any further because I was so pleased with the achievement and my time was limited.

I was certain people I knew would embrace my accomplishment; sadly that was not the case. I must have anticipated meeting with some disbelievers, but I never imagined the level of ridicule with which I was met. When the word got back to my father and his friends, I was further put down. My mother was the only one who gave me any credit, but I'm not sure she completely believed me. As I reflect on it today, I can understand how in the early 1950s my claims seemed utterly impossible.

But I went back to work with my horses and made them my life. During my childhood I lived in two distinctly separate worlds, one with horses, the other with people. My world with horses was one of comfort and understanding, but with people I felt isolated and alone.

•

It wasn't until early in 1985 that I attempted to demonstrate to my father the effectiveness of my work. I explained that what I was doing was based on what I learned out there in the desert. Even at that late date he was too set in his ways to give ground. Father and son relationships can be powerful and often inflexible, as ours was. There was never any give in the constant struggle for supremacy. My father tenaciously clung to his beliefs, and I to mine.

In February of 1997, I adopted three mustangs with the intention of repeating my experience of the 1950s. This time I was older and wiser, though somewhat less agile, and determined to record the event on film. Once again I confronted a wild mustang in the wilderness. I knew now that if I could persuade him to trust me I could cause him to accept his first saddle, bridle and rider without force or pain. Just as in 1951, Equus proved to be constant and reliable. It was incredibly tough for me, both physically and mentally, but this experience proved to be one of the most gratifying of my life.

The BBC/PBS television program about the mustang, which I named Shy Boy during that long twenty-four-hour ride through the Cuyama Valley of California when we became acquainted, was shown around the world. The video of that remarkable Join-Up became very popular when I conducted my lectures and demonstrations, and I often fielded remarks and questions about the event. One of the most frequently asked questions was, what did I think the mustang might do if he was taken back to the wild and turned loose? Would he go with the herd or return to me? It took more than a hundred queries of this kind before I realized that I had to accept another challenge.

By this time Shy Boy had been ridden for nearly a year and had been treated well. If I gave him the opportunity to choose between the wild horses and the wilderness or his newfound domestication and me, which would he choose? It was not without trepidation that Shy Boy was released to make his choice.

Come what may, I decided to document his release just as we had documented our first dramatic encounter. After we had tracked down the herd he knew before and released him, the wranglers who accompanied me, and the film crew, watched and waited, scanning the desert hills for any sign of his return. He had rejoined the herd without hesitation; they had welcomed him back before galloping off together. Through the remains of that day, and through the night, I watched him. In the early light of morning, we saw the herd on the crest of a hill. One horse stepped away from the others. I waited. Then Shy Boy came down the hill, galloping through the high grasses. Running directly to me, he put his head to my chest and, in the language of Equus, clearly stated that he was happy to be back with me. He had deliberately chosen to Join-Up with people over returning to his own kind.

I have always asserted that a happy horse that loves his work is better than one that has been forced. This has always been very difficult to demonstrate, but now for me there is no longer any question about it. A mustang, born into the world of absolute flight, chose caring people over his own kind. Shy Boy made his choice because I had gained his trust. Using his own language I had assured him that I was not predatorial and I'd made it clear to him that he could come to and stay with me without fear.

Body Language

Advance and Retreat

When I first encountered the wild mustangs in the Nevada desert as a boy, I also discovered how mustangs could be caught. The Indians from north of Battle Mountain introduced me to principles of advance and retreat. The wild herd is driven away from a trap (a keyhole-shaped structure made up of woven wire and posts, about a quarter of a mile long) for at least a day. You then ride back the other way and the herd tends to follow, leaving some riders to circle behind the herd and so complete the trap.

Advance and retreat was one of the first lessons taught to me by horses and I was later to discover that it works well with people, too. For the first time I realized that it was possible to converse with a wild horse. This was thrilling—not only was I discovering the presence of a wondrous language, but I was also discovering my own ability to decode it.

The flight animal's first reaction to a predator is to flee, using speed to escape from danger. With the attack safely averted, the flight animal will tend to stop, look back and reassess the situation. Survival of the fittest has taught the horse that the more he knows about his predator, the better he will be equipped to survive. In addition, it is critical to conserve energy. It makes little sense to run mindlessly into the jaws of another predator. A horse will often retrace his steps to the area of the attack to determine the nature of the predator, keeping track of its presence and appraising any current threat—somewhat along the lines of "better the devil you know . . ." This is the phenomenon known as "advance and retreat," and it is an essential part of the communication process. Humans also act out advance and retreat.

Consider the example of an adolescent boy just starting high school. He has a crush on a girl and follows her persistently. If the girl is not interested, she will ignore his advances. After some time his enthusiasm for this pursuit wanes. He loses interest and starts to look elsewhere. This is the moment when he takes the pressure off. It often does not take long before she misses his constant attention. In animal terms, he has been the predator and she the prey. She will notice he is no longer around and will feel his absence. She may not have had a crush on him, but she enjoyed his attentions. Perhaps she starts to appear where he is, or shows interest in him. Without consciously realizing it, she missed the pressure of his advances, which subconsciously made her aware of how good it felt to be wanted.

The clever salesman uses the principles of advance and retreat to make his commissions. First, he bombards the customer with attention and information and then he retreats, leaving the customer literally to miss the attention. The customer then contacts the salesman of his own volition. The moment that the salesman receives a voluntary approach from his prospective customer, he is metaphorically in the driver's seat. He can then use subtle tactics to convince his customer of the value of his product.

These concepts were made clear to me by horses over four decades. When the horse decides to approach me of his own volition, he is communicating that I have gone a long way toward selling him on how wonderful it might be to enter into a partnership.

Eyes on Eyes

The first gesture many predators make while stalking is to lock eyes on the eyes of the prey—there is no mistaking this for being anything but predatory. As soon as I release a horse in the round pen and he moves away from me, I lock my eyes on his eyes and take on an aggressive stance, my shoulders and body square to the horse. These actions alert the horse that I could be a predator and cause him to take flight.

A comparable situation occurs when a young man notices a girl he finds attractive and looks directly at her. The desire of one person for another can take on the nuances of a prey/predator scenario. If the female denies eye contact, it is very difficult for the relationship to develop. A relationship is apt to begin when there is eye-to-eye communication.

It is imperative that I am precisely aware of where I am looking at every moment during the process of Join-Up. I can actually slow a horse down by moving my point of vision along the horse's back toward his tail. The farther I focus away from his head, the slower the pace of the horse. I often show this when demonstrating Join-Up. Conversely, turning one's attention away is as important in this conversation as is a direct gaze. I always look down and away from the horse's eyes when I go in close to reward him by rubbing his forehead. By taking my eyes off the horse, I am taking the pressure off. The horse perceives the release of pressure as part of the reward.

Among humans eye contact also signals interest and communicates commitment. It maintains conversation. The lack of eye contact may very well be a natural, healthy and demonstrative part of the communication process. Cessation of that contact takes the pressure off and denotes a change in the flow of communication. The lack of eye contact can be interpreted in many ways. One might feel it demonstrates a lack of self-esteem and/or sincerity and the presence of confusion and/or fear.

Don't we demand that children should look at us when we are reprimanding them? The child often looks away and adults will generally consider this to show a lack of interest or even a passive defiance. How many times have we seen an angry parent grab a child's face and yell, "Look at me when I am talking to you!" From my experience with horses I feel that a child who looks away is passive and not dismissive. If a child stands square and drills the adult eye to eye, that child may well be accused of defiant behavior.

Autism

The language of the autistic child is similar to that of the flight animal, and his flight mechanism is far more finely tuned than that of a nonautistic child. The autistic child will almost never make eye-to-eye contact.

Autistic children are also acutely sensitive to body language. In a way similar to that of horses, they rely heavily on it for communication. So it is appropriate to briefly explore autism in this regard.

Autism is a neurological dysfunction that has many different levels of severity and whose cause is not entirely understood. Because the brain is a complex organ, any part or parts of it affected by disease or mutation can cause a wide variety of dysfunctions. What is clear is that the brain becomes overactive in certain areas, which could be a reaction to underdevelopment, or lack of development in other areas.

Autism is not a disease—one is simply born with the condition—and there is no dramatic cure. The word "autism" conveys to many of us a child or person locked into some strange world. Often mute, they seem inaccessible and removed from normality. Autistics are noted for their ability to concentrate deeply on some tiny aspect of their surroundings; they might lock onto a minute detail such as a pencil rolled between the fingers. They seem afraid and often hide from a direct gaze, finding odd corners to crouch in and immersing themselves in repetitive activity. Even less severe autistics can have difficulty relating to other people: they seem unable to read people well or to respond. They are people for whom the jigsaw of life is missing key pieces.

The autistic, like the horse, thinks spatially, or in pictures. Autistic people often find written language a struggle, and they mix up words and symbols for sounds and sometimes cannot even recognize specific sounds. However, autistics have the same range of intelligence as do nonautistic people. In fact, they are often very gifted in some areas while below par in others.

Recently there has been a considerable increase in horseback riding therapy centers where children with a wide range of disabilities can safely, under trained management, ride horses. Reports on the success of these ventures vary, but generally it is noticed that the act of riding is stimulating for autistic children. Riding provides the autistic child who is unable to walk with a freedom of movement over which he or she has some measure of control.

The close proximity of horse and rider also seems to be attractive to autistics and often helps to arrest violent or repetitive behavior. The child with high anxiety or suffering panic attacks almost instantly becomes calm once seated on a horse. The act of riding also helps the children to use muscles that would otherwise not be so actively employed and so their all-around development is enhanced while the sound of trees rustling, the feel of the wind in their faces and the smell of nature as they ride along combine to produce a complete and stimulating environment.

The horse and the autistic child have much in common. Noise, particularly loud and unusual sounds, can be terrifying to both. The horse thrives on routine, and autistics are almost fanatical about routine; one thing out of place and they are likely to throw a tantrum, which makes education very difficult and much communication depends upon body language.

A handshake might be perceived as an attack to such a child, who will often approach you from behind, just as the horse in my round pen does when I do Join-Up. Autistic children will try not to look you straight in the eye, but firm eye contact, conveying focus, plays an important part in their communication system, as does touch. Many such children want to be hugged but cannot handle the psychic distress that this stimulation causes. As with the horse a certain quality of touch is acceptable, but it must never be forced. Both will become very accustomed to seeing the outline of a person they deal with every day and will recognize familiar sounds and shapes. The horse is immediately alarmed when faced with something that has an unfamiliar shape and is liable to react with extreme fear, even spinning around and bolting. The autistic child will almost certainly fear strange sights or sounds, which can be a trigger to violent or repetitive behavior.

Perhaps it is not surprising that the horse, a visual thinker with an extraordinary ability to sense the intentions of its rider, is quite comfortable being ridden by autistics and, furthermore, is able to cope with their often unusual behavior.

My interest in autistic children is not entirely founded on the similarities they share with the horse. I also think in pictures, and perhaps this has something to do with my success in working with horses. For a long time it never occurred to me that everyone didn't think that way. I can still remember the floor plan of a house that my grandparents lived in—each room, how the furniture was arranged and where the windows were. That house was demolished when I was eighteen months old. When it came to designing Flag Is Up Farms, I had no difficulty in planning it out because I could see the end result. It was the same with our house and the subsequent alterations and extensions that I have made.

Temple Grandin is an autistic and a well-known author of several books and articles on her unusual life and chosen area of study—the design of feed lots, slaughterhouses, corrals and farms that handle animals. I first heard about her in the mid-1990s when her book *Thinking in Pictures* was recommended to me. I devoured it and was awestruck by the similarities that I found when comparing her thought processes to mine. I was impressed by her ability to recognize and reduce stress levels in cattle being handled in chutes. She used her special ability as an autistic with a pictorial memory to determine factors that terrified the cattle. She is now designing handling facilities for animals by employing concepts that would have been considered foolish and unnecessary just a couple of decades ago.

Temple Grandin has revolutionized the way in which cattle are brought to slaughter. Her autism means that she finds it difficult to cope with being touched and she fears loud and sudden noises, just as cattle do. So she brought a particular insight and sensibility to the problem of avoiding panic in cattle at stockyards. Her solution was simple, but brilliant: have the cattle follow a circular path, since moving in circles is in their nature and comforts them.

Though seemingly cut off from the world, the autistic may

have lessons to offer us. The ways of her fellow humans confound Temple Grandin but she saw something terribly lacking in the way we handle animals destined for human consumption. Her thinking has had a profound impact on the handling of cattle, sheep and swine all over the world.

Although I am not a vegetarian, I firmly believe that the handling of all animals destined for slaughter ought to be done with the primary objective of eliminating stress, trauma or pain.

I invited Ms. Grandin to join me at a demonstration in 1998. She is the only person who specializes in animal behavior whom I have ever allowed to take a microphone during my question-and-answer period and respond to my answers with comments of her own. This was a dangerous thing for me to do—there is a risk of being contradicted, or of disrupting my work with the raw horses. But I not only have confidence in my concepts, I have also come to respect her opinion. It turned out to be enjoyable and I would welcome the opportunity to do it again, but only with Temple Grandin. I felt this incredible sense of safety. In her response she is a flight animal, or as close to one as I have ever met. In my excitement at first meeting her that evening, I thrust out my hand and she ducked under the bleachers. Quickly, the horse trainer in me kicked in and I began to move more slowly and cautiously.

What Temple Grandin offers is a keen insight into what a flight animal goes through. "If you're a visual thinker," she once said, "it's easier to identify with animals." As an autistic, she has great difficulty understanding human emotions and codes of behavior; the touch of another human appeals intellectually to her but its physical aspects terrify and overwhelm her. Yet she reads the moods and signs of animals as she would a book. Cattle and autistics share common ground, because both are frightened by high-pitched sounds, sudden loud noises, air hissing. Temple Grandin understands very well why cattle fear shadows and sudden movements, how feeling and emotion is communicated by the body—even *through* the body and its movements.

In one of the many stories I heard about her, she actually entered a slaughterhouse chute when it was reported to her that cattle were stopping at a particular point. She had designed the facility, deploying circling ramps to calm the cattle, and everything was working fine except for this one problem. What she saw when she entered the chute was a chain hanging off to the left, maybe 20 feet away and 12 feet up in the air. The very slight swaying of that chain was stopping the cattle cold. The slaughterhouse officials had, at first, dealt with the problem by using an electric cattle prod. Temple was aghast at that and offered a better way: she had them wrap the chain in a leather pouch, which quieted both movement and sound, no longer distressing the cattle.

I respect Temple Grandin and her work immensely. I believe that the concepts she deals with on a daily basis also serve to validate my work.

Distractibility

A STORY

Cadillac

Recently an intern came to me at Flag Is Up Farms and said she thought that when I talked about a horse bringing baggage with him to the round pen that I was being melodramatic. She thought that it was highly unlikely that horses carried psychological baggage with them to new and different environments or relationships.

I explained to her that the flight animal, with its two goals in life—one to reproduce and the other to survive—is far quicker to collect and store psychological baggage than even we human beings. Reproduction aside, their life is led and driven by their incredible skills to survive; they simply don't have that much else to think about. An incident that frightened a horse and caused it concern about its surviving is apt to be logged in the brain so cleverly that it can be called up years later as a warning should the horse believe himself once again in trouble.

Cadillac was such a horse. I was doing some work for a friend, gathering and sorting cattle. I was riding at a brisk trot down a narrow lane that was fenced on either side. I noticed a bush growing in the fence line on my left side, but it didn't bother me. I was relaxed and standing in my stirrups, but as I rode past the bush, a pig bolted out, crossing in front of us. Before I knew what happened, Cadillac exploded and bucked me off.

A young, inexperienced horse, Cadillac had decided he had to get rid of me quickly as he prepared himself to survive the oncoming attack from the most frightening creature he had ever laid his eyes on.

I kept Cadillac for several years after that and as once or twice a year I had a chance to visit my friends I would trot down that same lane. I know I watched that bush with far greater interest than I had that first day, but so did Cadillac. The first time we returned it took us nearly ten minutes to pass the bush. By the eighth or tenth visit we could pass the bush but not without Cadillac snorting and moving way over, giving it as wide a berth as possible. Cadillac would have viewed that bush with suspicion for the rest of his life had he continued to return to that lane.

This is "baggage." It comes in many forms. It is deep-seated or shallow. But my experience with horses tells me clearly that if the frightening or traumatic incident is major, then the memory is more securely imprinted. My experience with horses has also taught me that if there is pain involved with the experience, it is indelibly etched in their memories. The same applies to human beings, both children and adults.

•

There are parallels between the way in which horses and other animals perceive the world around them and the way humans see and record information. By understanding these parallels we can gain a greater understanding of why people and animals react to situations as they do. By understanding how they communicate we can better interpret human communication.

To survive in the wild, a horse must be aware of everything happening around him at all times. He cannot allow a lion or wolf to creep up on him and make a surprise attack. Animals that are preyed upon must always be on their guard and aware of every element of their environment. Everyone who rides or works with horses knows that they can startle at the slightest thing, a paper bag in a bush, a sudden noise, a shadow or the appearance of a strange object. Once the horse has become aware of potential danger he will focus on it, but never to the extent that he ignores the rest of his environment. In human terms this could be described as being distractible.

An animal that must hunt for food in the wild can only survive if it understands the environment it is in. It needs to be aware of everything going on around it at any one moment—such awareness could mean the difference between life and death: if it were focused too deeply on one thing it might not notice an impending attack. In such situations it is actually important to be easily distracted, to be able to hear and be aware of everything going on. In such a context, distractibility, or the ability to be totally aware of your environment, is a valuable asset. However, in the modern human world this can be a handicap; human beings often need to be able to focus on one thing, excluding everything else. It is important for the student to be able to block out the distractions of the classroom and concentrate on the task at hand.

In fact the distractible child is at a grave disadvantage in the schoolroom and is often misunderstood. When the other children are concentrating on studies, the distractible child may have his or her attention drawn off by some minor detail no one else is aware of. The result is a slowness to learn and to complete exams and tests. Teachers often mistake distractibility for an absence of interest in the subject matter or perceive the child's wandering interest as a reflection on their own inability to teach, and it can be the cause of bad relations between child and teacher.

Many children suffer from this. It is not that they will not focus on one thing—they simply cannot. At the extreme level, autistic people can find screening out peripheral sounds and distractions almost impossible, and for some the external cacophony can become a nightmare—their only defense is to retract into some other world, closing off from the people and distractions around them.

The horses taught me the advantage of their natural distractibility, both for themselves and for humans. Anyone running a household needs to be constantly aware of many things going on around them as they raise children and see to the hundred and one jobs around the home; and it is a valuable talent to be able to walk into an office, pick up on several things happening at the same time and then pass on that information. Distractible children are likely to be good at team games like football where an ability to concentrate on many things at the same time is a useful attribute. As thinking in pictures allowed Temple Grandin to develop her designs for handling animals, so distractibility should be regarded as a useful trait and not condemned in the classroom simply because it reduces the child's efficiency to study.

Reading Each Other

Horses are flight animals and we need to start where they are—start by understanding as best we can their history and experience. Communicating with a troubled human being or a skeptical young flight animal is difficult to do even when we labor at it in an exemplary fashion. If I try to insist that my horse learn quickly to understand communication at the level I understand it, he will often be reticent and resentful. I believe that people are no different. I feel strongly that we need to move philosophically to their level of understanding and then work slowly toward what we perceive to be our goal.

Human beings often fail to clearly observe one another's body language. The story of George Simpson is about two men taking a chance on each other and learning to communicate and respect each other. It is about a young man who brought a lot of personal problems to a relationship, but learned to step away from them without negatively impacting the lives around him.

Early one morning back in the seventies on my way to the farm mechanic's shop, I saw a pickup with a camper shell on the back. It was parked off to one side and I assumed it belonged to one of the farm workers. As I looked on, the door opened at the back of the camper and a tall, lean young man got out.

"Can I help you?" I offered.

"I'm George Simpson," he said, "from Lincoln, Nebraska."

George appeared to me to be about twenty years of age. He said he was looking for work.

"What can you do?" I inquired.

He replied that he was from a farming family and could do just about anything on a farming operation.

"Did you just drive in and park your truck here hoping to get a job?"

"Yep. That is what I did."

I asked if he had thought about making an application for work. He didn't know about making applications, but what he knew was that he had a lot of trouble at home, that he was good at farm work and needed a job. He said he had no problems with the law, just with his dad and he didn't want to talk about them.

Country boys just don't leave the family farm without a strong reason. But I had a strong inner feeling that George just might be honest and competent. My personal background and the experience of working with many young people had taught me to read situations like this. George made it clear to me that he had experienced very serious problems with his father. I surmised that he perceived their relationship was unacceptable and filled with anguish. It was a very bold move for such a young man to uproot and drive halfway across the country with no job prospect in sight. I was concerned with the amount of emotional baggage George brought with him, but I had made up my mind to take a chance.

I felt strongly that what George needed was someone to trust him. Someone to set him free so that he could use his talent and experience in order to produce. He needed to know that there was confidence in him and that it was okay to take some risks and to innovate. I felt comfortable playing that role and from very early on in our relationship I sensed a feeling of contentment had come over him.

I asked my farm foreman to give him a job and we put him to work. All that day I watched him out of the corner of my eye to see if he would fit into the operation. He was clearly knowledgeable about the agricultural equipment we used on the farm. He had obviously been raised with it and handled it competently. Later we went to the house where I fixed dinner and he ate like a starving lion. When I asked him, he admitted he hadn't eaten for three days, which was about as long as it would have taken him to drive from Nebraska to Solvang.

We gave him a permanent job and it wasn't long before he became the natural choice for foreman. He is probably responsible for more good things around this farm than almost anybody who has worked on it before or since. George moved into the bunkhouse, which had two rooms and was very minimal. He set out enlarging it to what was eventually a five-bedroom house. Among the improvements to the farm were flood-control projects, a new road and building the breeding barns. He did a lot of work to improve the pastures and the race track.

He was with us for about twelve years. There wasn't a day that George did not give 100 percent to his job. At no time during his tenure did I ever find reason to question his honesty, his integrity or his loyalty. His work ethics were absolutely solid gold.

Later in George's tenure he confided to me that the reason he had left home was because the relationship between him and his father was not good. His father had a lot of trouble coping with an adult son whom he saw primarily as a threat to his position on the farm. They had bitter fights. George loved the Nebraska farm, but he knew he had to leave it to get on with his life. While he felt his father loved him, it seemed it was just too difficult to bring his son into the family farming operation.

George had been working for us about seven years before he felt comfortable talking to me about home life. It was also then that he confided to me that his mother had informed him his father had developed the early stages of Alzheimer's disease. It was decided that he should bring his father out to California to relieve the situation at home.

His father did come, but problems were grave. His father would drive into Buellton, a mile and a half away, and would not be able to find his way back. The pressure on the family was extreme and finally it was decided that George's parents should take an apartment near Lincoln and give up farming. George was now suddenly free to go home and take over running the farm, no longer threatened by his father.

I was of course totally supportive of his decision, but in my heart devastated at the loss of such a wonderful friend and worker. George was in every way an exemplary employee. He remains remembered in all the projects he accomplished.

Recently George and his wife attended one of my demonstrations. It was wonderful to see him again and it was as though I were visiting with a long lost cousin that I was extremely fond of. George is the kind of person each of us wants to know. He is bright, but quiet, warm and friendly. I will always admire him deeply.

THE ROUND PEN

The catch-pen's dust was the beginning—the beginning of the day's work and most of the evening's reflections.
LEA AINSWORTH AND KENNETH W. DAVIS,
The Catch Pen

When a young, unstarted horse enters the round pen he is stepping into the unknown and his adrenaline is up. The success of my method is based on my ability to communicate with the horse, and the round pen provides me with a controlled environment in which intense conversation can take place. Traditionally, however, it has been used for a very different purpose.

I didn't invent the idea of the round pen. In pioneer days it was often made of logs, interlaced to create a circular enclosure. The round pen became a part of nearly every ranching outfit in western North America. They go a long way back in cowboy lore. You will see them in the paintings of Charles Russell, Frederic Remington, Edward Borein or more recently, J. N. Swanson. I have seen round pens with walls made of huge logs, others with plank fences or concrete blocks or a single strand of electrified tape, and some that had been dug out of the ground with the earth as their walls. I know of round pens made of discarded trucking pallets, used tires and railroad ties, even bales of hay: virtually every building material that one can conjure.

Most of the round pens of the old West had a very large tree trunk standing in the center, with deep grooves worn into it by the ropes that were used to restrain the wildest animals you can imagine. A couple of wraps around this snubbing post could cause a wild horse to come crashing to the ground literally at the end of his tether. The round pen was the classroom for "traditional horse breaking." Horses were restrained, blindfolded and broken to submission.

The ranch horse generally faced his first days of domestication in the round pen. You could call it a kindergarten of sorts for those untrained animals who needed to learn how to comply with the wishes of man. It was also a place of injury and death, as many equine lives were lost during the breaking process, and many horses sustained injuries severe enough to cause their destruction. The lives of horsemen were lost in round pens as well and injuries to them occurred in far too great a number to chronicle. I remember seeing a round pen in northern Nevada, where an old rancher had created a tradition of painting black and white crosses on the planks. The white crosses were for cowboys who died; the black crosses were for horses. It wasn't very fair, this battle of wills. I can't recall the exact number of black crosses—I think there were thirty or so, but I remember being transfixed by the three white crosses at the far left end of one plank. They stood out like neon against the darkened wood. The planks had endured more winters and summers than the old cowboy cared to remember.

These marks symbolized what I believed to be an unnecessary

tragedy. Round pens are simple enclosures and the activities conducted within them can be harsh or gentle, just as many instruments in the horse world can be dangerous or harmless. Horse equipment is only as good as the hands that use it. Although the traditional training of horses often used methods I consider brutal, some horsemen were far more humane.

The round pen itself is an ingenious configuration. It allows the animal to move without stopping the flow of energy, as an enclosure with corners would do. It also allows the person directing the activity to travel a lesser distance than the horse, which is necessary given the physical superiority of the equine student. On Flag Is Up Farms I have several round pens of various designs. I have taken great pains to study the construction of these enclosures because they provide me with the optimum environment within which the horse can learn.

It *is* possible to Join-Up with a mustang in the wild where there are no round pens, fences or boundaries. I have achieved that a few times in my life, and as I have described none more dramatically than when I joined-up with Shy Boy in the Cuyama Valley of California. The context was so vastly different from that of a round pen that, in order to succeed, I had to prepare myself to accept the fact that the Join-Up would require a great deal more time than when operating in a round pen environment. It made no sense to enter a project such as this in the wilderness thinking I could achieve Join-Up in thirty minutes. That would sentence the project to certain failure. I spent weeks preparing myself and my horses for what was going to be a long and very difficult task: by changing the context so dramatically, I would have to significantly modify the process. If I was to achieve my goal it would have to be through innovation.

The round pen is the place where two entities come together; at first they are disconnected, but then with proper discourse they become harmonious and synchronized. Communication takes place there and enables learning. There is no such thing as teaching, only learning. Knowledge cannot be pushed into a brain; it must be willingly drawn into the brain by the recipient. This can be achieved by creating an environment in which a horse or a person can learn by choice—the schools, colleges, universities and businesses of the world need to create such an atmosphere. The round pen means many things to my horse and me. It is a classroom where the basic educational elements germinate, like well-nurtured seeds. It can be a boardroom for negotiating contracts, where I convince my equine student that he should allow me to chair the meeting. I don't want him to be subservient, nor to perceive that he is—I want it to be a partnership, but someone must call the shots.

In most circumstances a horse comes into this environment with deep-seated distrust, fear and anxiety. I create change through communication, so that these fears are replaced with trust and acceptance. Metaphorically, I always keep the door open. It's unimportant if the response I get is not the one desired. The horse is saying, "I am willing to look at this contract." Any response at all should be viewed in a positive light as a portal through which you can pass to create positive or negative consequences and thus begin the process of negotiation.

When an untrained horse enters the round pen he is in a strange place, with a human present, no other horses and no obvious escape route. His only goal is survival.

If at this point the human communicates that he is not predatorial, the horse is able to assess calmly what is available to him. His keen senses are in their most heightened state, and with 50 million years of experience to draw upon he instinctively sets out to negotiate with his human counterpart in an effort to come out alive. If the human knows the language of Equus he is then able to create an environment for learning. He can offer leadership and ask the horse if he would like to join his herd.

In a round pen the flight route keeps the horse at a steady pace around the perimeter of the pen. The horse can flee from me, but his flight will bring him back to the place he started from.

The round pen helps me to achieve the first stage of our conversation. It creates the context in which our conversation takes place, and the context of any meeting can affect the speed of the outcome. Within the controlled environment of the round pen, I can initiate responses from the horse. As I ask and respond to the horse's signals, I never lose sight of my objective, which is to ask the horse to willingly allow itself to be saddled, bridled and ridden. This is achieved through "objective listening" or "amplified reflection." The trainer must always remain objective and should not personalize the horse's responses. Abuse is more apt to occur when a trainer perceives that he is personally under attack.

I have often observed horse trainers who acted out violently against their equine student. They shout and curse saying things like, "He's evil and his mother was the same way." "The idiot is just plain crazy and he'll get somebody killed if I don't show him who is boss."

Of course, none of these things is true. No flight animal can contrive to act against you. Each of its actions is a response to something the trainer has done. The trainer has perceived the actions of the horse to be directed against him personally. Knowing no other alternative, he acts out violently. The trainer has been taught by generations of predecessors that it is necessary to physically break the will of the horse.

People can contrive to be difficult, but close observation will show that most prefer to get along with one another. Obstreperous behavior is most often a response to actions that negatively impacted them.

My round pen is a place where I introduce to the horse the idea that he and I are on the same team. The horse has a natural understanding of the concept of the herd and teamwork. How often can the same be said about people?

•

When I first met Queen Elizabeth II, I have to admit I was nervous. I had been asked to demonstrate my Join-Up technique in the riding school at Windsor Castle. When I was introduced to the royal family, my pulse rate shot up. Only the day before I had been taken by Sir John Miller, the queen's equerry, to see the round pen I would be using for my demonstration. It was a wire mesh pen, solidly made and linked in sections. Okay, I suppose, but I had never started a horse in one of this type before. I didn't know if it would work, and to add to the problems I already faced, there would be people sitting around the outside of the pen in full view of the horse. I had no idea how that would affect Join-Up. I have never started a horse with my adrenaline as high as it was that day after being introduced to Her Majesty. I was subjecting myself to a considerable change in context: a wire mesh pen, people all around the outside and a heartbeat like an express train.

But once I stepped into the pen and started working with the horse, I realized that this new environment was not going to affect my ability to communicate or that of the horse. The moment our work began I could feel my pulse rate returning to normal. The fact that I could so easily override my nervousness in this tense environment showed me the power of my relationship with horses. The queen notwithstanding, I was in my element.

In fact, if the quality of communication is adequate, the outcome will probably be satisfactory. All the same, the context of any meeting—the place in which you work, the office in which you hold a meeting—can affect the outcome.

The fact that I overcame the significant distractions of the environment in which I was asked to work surprised me greatly upon reflection. The reason for my surprise is that I know full well the importance of a comfortable environment when it comes to producing top-of-the-line work. I have often worked in won-

Monty and Pat riding above Flag is Up Farms in the early 1970s.
Overleaf: Monty working as a camp counsellor at Douglas Summer Camp in 1954.

Above: Monty and Pat releasing the first horses at Flag is Up Farms in 1966.

Below: Roberts family, 1967. Left to right are Pat, Laurel, Debbie, Monty and Marty.

Above: Marty and Monty at a father–son night at Santa Ynez Valley High School, where Marty played football.

Right: Steve Arellano, a former foster child of Monty and Pat's who returned to Flag is Up for his wedding to Sherry – he is part of the Roberts extended family.

Above: A proud Monty with his first grandson Matthew, son of his daughter Debbie and her husband Tom Loucks.

Left: Monty and Pat at home.

Right: Monty and Shy Boy demonstrate their unusual friendship to an audience of children.

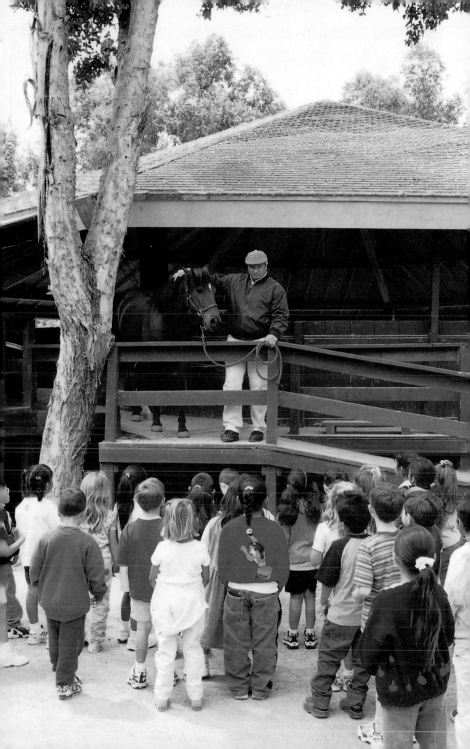

Above: The audience around the round pen at a demonstration of Join-Up in Australia.

Below: Monty demonstrates the blind trust walk – an exercise employed during training events at Flag is Up to teach the importance of developing a trust-based relationship.

derful surroundings with facilities properly designed for efficient output and believe me, I have much more confidence in the outcome when this is the case. Where my equine and human students are concerned, normally speaking, the better my surroundings, the more successful we are.

WHY WE NEED JOIN-UP

All the remedial horses that are brought to me are carrying the baggage of physical and emotional abuse, real or perceived. Even after I have worked with them and restored them to a more normal state, the baggage they carry always remains just under the surface for the rest of their lives. I include emotional abuse because a horse can suffer severe damage from confused messages given to it during training by people who simply do not understand what they are doing. Horses do become confused and worried, not only because they have been beaten or whipped, but also from mixed signals that just as easily destroy the horses' confidence.

When I was a child I observed horses being broken. I watched as they were tied down, and abused in most appalling ways. I sensed that there was something profoundly wrong in this. I believed that the horse had absolutely no idea what was expected of it. It was painful to me to see what I perceived to be confusion on the faces of these horses. I had been treated harshly as well and I felt acute empathy for them. My father was never going to understand me, but I wanted more than anything for the horses to have the chance I would never get. At that time I doubted that I would be fully understood but I wanted the horses to have a chance to live without brutality. It was a vague and distant goal. It was not formulated or defined, but one I was determined to achieve. I have dedicated my life to it. As I continue to work with horses their language becomes clearer and it is clear that horses, like children, desperately want to be loved, understood and accepted.

Questions are the basis of our communication. Imagine a world of people who are incapable of asking questions. Children who cannot communicate are at a huge social disadvantage. Virtually all parents have experienced a time with their children when they are inundated with questions. Why this? Why that? Answering these questions is essential for the child to find its place in the universe. Without answers the child begins the rest of his life without direction.

The same applies to horses. We tell them to do things for us, expecting them to understand what we are saying. With little or no training, we expect them to know our language or respond to our commands. We tend to demand and not request. We tend to use painful punishment if we don't get an immediate response. We assume that our language is the only language. We are wrong.

The Whoa Rope

One way the traditional horseman teaches a horse to stop is with the "whoa rope," also known as the "Running W." The "whoa rope" is usually about thirty-five feet long and is attached to the horse in such a way that pulling on one end of it elevates the horse's two front feet up to his chest. The trainer then sends the horse away at speed. As he approaches the end of the rope, the trainer yells "Whoa" and tugs his end of the rope. The horse's front feet are locked to his chest and he comes crashing to the ground, often hitting his muzzle. Legs are sometimes broken and teeth are knocked out, but after eight or ten repetitions of the procedure, the horse will stop when the trainer yells "whoa." That is, if it is still healthy enough to do so.

Such traditional methods are still used in many places around the world. In the late thirties and early forties, I was an eyewitness to this kind of brutality, not only in training facilities but also in the movie industry. The "whoa rope" procedure was outlawed in films in the early fifties and things have changed for the better since then. It should be obvious that any horse that has been subjected to this treatment is going to carry around the memory of the fear and pain associated with the word "whoa." The same could be said of pain inflicted by whip or spur. There is no partnership here; it is domination. When I say "Whoa!" I just want my horse to stop; I don't want it to relive feelings of pain and domination.

When I start to work with a damaged or remedial horse, I watch its responses to my body language, so as to piece together a picture of the kind of abuse or mishandling the horse has been subjected to. Some owners genuinely don't know what has happened to their horse; others conceal certain embarrassing facts. It doesn't matter; the horses do the talking. They tell me where they have been abused and with what level of violence, and they clearly demonstrate their attitude to the abuse. People react in contrasting ways to similar situations: some return abuse to their abusers with increased violence, and others suffer quietly and transform that abuse into anxiety and paranoia.

Join-Up, on the other hand, facilitates learning. With Join-Up horses have the advantage of being able to communicate with me and to understand my goals for them. I believe this is why they learn at a rate thought by many to be impossible. I am often met with skepticism by traditional horsemen, but even they can be won over in the end, given enough information they can't ignore. Once you have a horse's trust you can begin the long road of reschooling, of overlaying his previous experience by giving him positive reward for positive actions. Join-Up is the key to achieving a proper level of communication.

IMPRINTING OUR YOUNG

Most of the emotional baggage people carry around with them, at home or in the workplace, comes from their childhood. The real damage to the psyche of a child is done in what I call the 0–1 time frame (birth to kindergarten).

In the rearing of horses, foal imprinting is brilliantly simple and effective, primarily because it falls into the 0–1 time frame. Foal imprinting is a process developed by Dr. Robert Miller, a renowned veterinarian and equine behaviorist. As soon as the foal is born, the mother imprints it through nuzzling and licking—she bonds with it. Bonding with the human child is an equally important factor between mother and baby. It is possible to introduce the foal to human contact through imprinting during the first hour of its life. Nature has created a tiny window of opportunity at this point in time, when the youngster logs memories that are virtually indelible. A good experience with a human being at this point creates a trust that has the potential to last a lifetime. The same applies to many species. Cat and dog lovers will tell you how important it is to handle newborns.

At Flag Is Up Farms and at the Monty Roberts Learning Center, we begin the imprinting process before the foal has even cleared the birth canal. We massage sensitive areas such as the head, ears, mouth, neck, back and foreflanks. We handle the feet and the legs. Spending twenty-five minutes at this critical time in the young horse's life can in fact virtually eliminate behavioral problems in the life of the horse. We follow up this initial imprinting with two or three more sessions in the first ten days or so.

We are careful never to interfere with the mother-offspring bonding. Similar bonding in humans has similar results but that is only part of the story, because a baby needs more than an hour of bonding. The child who has been loved and given quality time will have plenty of emotional resources in reserve when times are hard, whereas the child who was starved of love early on will quickly succumb to life's pressures and, just like a damaged horse, will very easily develop attitude problems, particularly when faced with confusion and mixed messages.

My concepts help to reestablish a positive pattern of behavior. Good is rewarded and negative actions result in extra tasks. If you are consistent and caring and never use any emotional blackmail, higher standards of behavior can be achieved. However, the potential for failure is never far from the surface. Certainly, with an abused horse or person one violent act could easily set you back years in your work. Every time you break trust it becomes harder to build it up again, but it is nearly always possible to regain if you are willing to change your approach.

By contrast, I suspect that it would be fair to say that most of the remedial horses that I work with were damaged later in life than in the 0–1 time frame, with one memorable exception: a horse that became one of the most dangerous animals with which I have dealt.

A STORY

Barlet

Disney Studios was looking for a flashy palomino foal to use in the film *The Horse with the Flying Tail.* Slim Pickens, the actor, found a delightful foal called Barlet. Slim played with the foal and taught him to retrieve sticks. When Barlet returned with the object, Slim would playfully lift the foal's forelegs onto his shoulders.

With their size and athleticism, horses can become extremely dangerous if inappropriate behavior is encouraged. Barlet, in that critical early period of his life, had been given significant positive reward for negative actions. Can you imagine the danger a handler might face once Barlet was a full-sized adult horse weighing more than 1,000 pounds? Any time he executed his front-legs-on-shoulders routine, a person was immediately at risk of either serious injury or death. A monster had been created.

Barlet was shown in conformation competition throughout the western United States. While he was a major champion, he had become so dangerous to handle that he had to be kept in a box stall equipped with an electrically charged wire to keep him from tearing the walls down. Whenever the charge on the wire surrounding his stall was disconnected, the horse turned into a tiger.

I was offered half ownership of Barlet if I could get him into the show ring in San Francisco where the 1964 Grand National was being held. He had won his age class and needed to go back into the ring for the championship for stallions of all ages. Since Barlet's value was in the five-figure range, I thought it was worth a try. I was also excited by the challenge and thought there was no horse I couldn't handle!

I began the retraining program that I have used on so many horses, offering positive reinforcement for positive action. With Barlet it worked, but it created only a thin veneer that often broke. He remained deeply disturbed. I trained him until his death, but he was chronically distrustful and mentally unstable, almost psychopathic, a horse made mean by people with good intentions.

•

Give people, especially children, enough of the wrong responses and they can easily be made mean. Horses aren't born mean; neither are people. Barlet carried baggage of the worst kind. He was affected so early that it was impossible to completely eliminate his deep-seated negative behavioral traits.

Abused children can fall into the Barlet bracket. If the abuse, whether emotional or physical, occurs early on, it imprints the worst possible message to the child—a message so indelible that only the deepest therapy can touch it, and in many cases little or nothing can be done.

Three

AGAINST VIOLENCE

Violence is the last refuge
of the incompetent.
—ISAAC ASIMOV

I mentioned before that I have a strong inclination to start and end
every segment of this book with the following three statements:

Violence is never the answer.

Violence is always for the violator
and never for the victim.

No one of us was born with the right to say
"you must or I'll hurt you"
to any other creature, animal or human.

These principles are the strongest lesson that horses have taught
me. I say that because horses were at least my primary teachers
and have actively and literally educated me. Let us take a look at
what is meant by these words:

Violence is never the answer.
We human beings cannot solve our problems by acting violently toward any other creature. We use violence in an attempt to answer or respond to our problems, but not until we communicate and negotiate with others in a tranquil and civil manner do we truly gain the solutions we are seeking.

Violence is for the violator and never for the victim.
Violators act through a sense of frustration. They reach a point at which they feel they are without choices. They go into an aggressive mode and attempt to bash their subject into agreement. If we are in conflict with one another, the most positive results are always obtained if we can agree to enter into negotiations that will ultimately produce solutions to the dilemma.

No one of us was born with the right to say "You must or I'll hurt you" to any other creature, animal or human.
This statement outlines my core belief that to force others to comply with our wishes is inhumane and immoral. I do not believe that nature intended for us to act in this manner.

All of this raises the question, "How do you define violence?" It's a very difficult question with no simple answer. I am, however, very clear about the kinds of violence that I abhor, so I'd like to take you through a few different scenarios, since violent acts can be categorized differently sometimes, depending on one's point of view.

The lion attacks the antelope, knocks it to the ground and breaks its neck with its jaws, killing it instantly. Is that an act of violence? In my opinion, it is not. It is an act of nature, conducted to sustain one species through the loss of an individual of another species, which nature has provided as if for that purpose.

A man walks up to a woman who works with him in the same company. The man shouts at the woman, "You're ugly and horrible. I can't stand the sight of you." This to me is a violent act. Extreme verbal abuse can, indeed, be very destructive; it's a point women often make to me during my sessions on tour. "I would almost prefer it," they say, "if the man would just go ahead and hit me. It wouldn't hurt nearly as much as some of the verbal abuse that I suffer." Verbal abuse can be cutting, degrading and often leaves indelible scars—it has the potential to be as damaging as physical violence. A father who ridicules a daughter for being too fat is engaging in a violent act that often produces long-term negative effects, some of which can be fatal. Many teenage eating disorders have their roots in belittling, destructive statements.

What about the guy running on a grassy field? He is dressed in strange clothes all of a dark color. He sees a man coming his way who is dressed in white. He runs as fast as he can toward the man, ramming into him and knocking him to the earth. Is this a violent act? No, providing that there are white lines on the grass and each of the men is a member of a competing football team. Providing that the action was within the prescribed rules, then it was agreed to bilaterally. Each person knew what was expected when he came on the field and chose to be there. But if the man in dark clothes gets up and steps on the face of his opponent, then this is a very violent act. The coach who encourages violence outside the agreed rules of the game not only misses the essence of the competition, but introduces an element of serious irresponsibility. And I would argue that this will ultimately cost him efficiency within his team on the field and therefore he will lose more games than he will win.

I played football for a national championship team, Hartnell College. It was in the division of two-year colleges, but the performance was at an extremely high level. I know the value of a tough competitor and playing the game with intense dedication, but violence for violence's sake was discouraged by all coaching staff.

A lady came to me in Kentucky in the summer of 1999. She

had a question about her son who, as a junior at high school, was active in the soccer program. He had wanted to play football for some time, but she had discouraged this. When he became a junior, she said that he could play football if he got better grades. He apparently worked very hard, improved his grades significantly and was given the chance to join the football team. The mother described to me the first day she went to his practice, saying that she heard the coach yelling at the kids, "You hit him like he was your worst enemy! Knock him down and give him a knee in the ribs as you get up." He told them he wanted them to consider their opponents as trash: "Treat them with contempt. You have to go after them like you believe they are the worst people on earth or you won't get mean enough to play this game." The mother told me she was very disturbed by all this and sorry that her son was involved in this kind of sport.

My response was that she was absolutely right to be incensed by this form of coaching. Every parent should get involved in those activities that help form the core beliefs of the children. I too was incensed when I came across people who coach in this fashion. It is unfair to the sport to imply that it condones this mentality. Young players can become even more effective on the playing field if they respect their opponent, play the game hard, but live within the framework of the rules and view with pride the methods by which they meet the task.

•

Violence comes in many forms, and most of those who study violent criminal behavior will agree that the perpetrator of violent acts against other human beings later in life is often guilty of abusing animals early on. To hurt a defenseless animal is probably one of the most cowardly acts that any human can perpetrate. The horse is a herbivore and the species is approximately fifty million years old. There is no evidence that it has ever stalked, killed or devoured another animate object—it is a grazer with no intention of causing harm to any other animals. If we examined what horses have endured at the hands of humankind in an effort to control and enslave them, it would sicken any caring individual. It is curious to note the rarity with which other species stalk or kill except to sustain their own life, yet man often acts with lethal violence, often without the justification of self-defense.

Family violence is on the increase—marital abuse and the killing of women by their husbands are a tragedy of our society that we're failing to control; the abuse of children continues despite efforts to the contrary—they are insufficient; and in North America we are seeing a frightening rise in school violence, the most notorious perhaps being the massacre at Columbine.

THE ROAD TO COLUMBINE

I ask each of the horses that I work with to allow me to pick up its feet one at a time. The main reason for this is that I want the horse to give up its weapons to me. The feet are the primary weapons of the equine anatomy. In human terms it is difficult to have a trusting relationship until we are willing to give up our weapons.

What motivated the two boys responsible for the Columbine High School shootings, in which thirteen people were killed? The answer to the problem certainly is not more police and metal detectors. We are now striving to learn all the factors that developed the characters of these two boys that resulted in the tragedy. I am frustrated by the reaction of well-meaning people who indicate surprise that it occurred. Why should we be surprised that this or any similar occurrences have taken place? As a society we have engineered and very carefully created the environment where this type of destructive behavior is inevitable, where children can kill, and then kill themselves.

Plato believed that people exposed to negative images try to duplicate the actions shown in such images. Therefore, Plato was opposed to the arts. He felt that the arts inflamed the emotions, causing people to act in irrational ways.

Plato professed that emotions should always be subordinate to reason. When the emotional/reasoning hierarchy becomes disturbed, the predicted result is what we see on our television news programs each day: a chaotic society ruled by impulse and instant gratification.

Over the last thirty years we've set out to foster certain traits, which are key in forming the behavioral patterns of young people. We have, for instance, created a cable television network on which we have consciously supported many channels devoted to the twenty-four-hour airing of movies. A quick survey of these channels on any given night reveals that most of them will be running movies in which dozens of people are being killed in scene after scene. The incredible effort that is expended in finding new and more exciting ways to commit violent acts is overwhelming. We are inundated with scene after scene striving to impress on us that violence can be the answer to a given problem, or that there is good violence and bad violence. Most "action movies" confusingly encourage young people to applaud their hero for blowing up a building or mowing down a few thousand people and boo the villain for doing virtually the same thing.

Much of the credit for our species' survival as hunter/gatherers must go to our ability to stalk, kill and devour. There was a time when our ability to reason and communicate meant less than our ability to dominate. We are having a hard time developing into a civilized society without need for physical superiority. Many argue that our innate appetite for violence can be satisfied in a vicarious fashion, that those of us who buy tickets to professional wrestling, boxing, football and the martial arts are answering that call.

Then there is the matter of behavior: another disturbing characteristic of many action films is to endow heroes with celebrity status and encourage young viewers to see as acceptable truly atrocious human behavior.

It was appalling that the news media exposed the existence of the videotapes made by the two perpetrators of the Columbine atrocity and allowed them to be shown on national television. Was it surprising that those two boys named the most influential computer games as their role models? That one of these teenagers showed a shotgun that he intended to use in the killings and announced that it was named after a prominent character in a video game? It was chilling to hear. I read the names of the Hollywood directors the boys predicted would be fighting over their story, to realize these boys were willing to slaughter others and kill themselves for a piece of the celebrity that we have all held out to be so desirable. Is this not verification of the result of giving positive consequences for negative actions?

It is easy to blame the entertainment industry for the content we criticize, but it would not exist if our society did not want it. We consciously buy theater tickets and turn on the television set. We clearly decide where we go and what we watch. The entertainment industry only responds to our demands. We make the rules; we create the market.

The most important rule governing my concepts is that we are responsible for our own actions and the consequences of our actions. So we can choose to stop overt, violent entertainment very quickly. We can choose to be aware of the examples we offer children.

For example, consider a mother with two young boys. One is twelve, the other is nine. You hear the mother say to the twelve-year-old, "Johnny, stop hitting your little brother or I am going to hit you." What sort of message could this possibly send except that when Johnny is bigger than his mother, it's okay for Johnny to hit her? It presupposes that violence is a logical response when in fact it is not. Or when Johnny learns to use a weapon, will he not then take pleasure in shooting his teachers from a tower? Or perhaps a physically superior athlete in his high school? Violence will almost always return to you in a similar form.

I found it amazing that within a few days after the Columbine school incident, certain people appeared on television saying that the motion picture industry was not at fault; others said that the video games were not at fault; there were those who eliminated any fault from parents; there were those who exonerated the gun-producing industry. We all stood up to claim "not guilty"; it is obvious that we all are.

Along with thousands of young Americans of my generation, I was raised with a gun case filled with shotguns, rifles and ammunition. I was taught from an early age that they were never to be pointed at another human being in jest or otherwise. It is the attitude with which we deal with dangerous instruments and not the fact they are dangerous instruments that really matters. But I am not saying that we should exonerate the gun-making industry from responsibility: in fact, we should, in my opinion, immediately ban all assault weapons.

Our society is ineffective in its attempts to reduce violence. The prison systems that the "civilized world" has adopted in the past century are wrong in their approach to correcting negative behavioral patterns. You should not incarcerate a young human being, tell him to mix with other lawbreakers for several years and then put him back out in society expecting him to behave in an acceptable manner. How can such a system work? One of the most important social institutions we should examine with a view to improving is the trash bin into which we put offenders—the prisons.

Nothing will happen to improve the situation unless the underlying philosophy of correction is changed. People who break the law owe society something in return—they should be ex-

pected to work to repay their debt to society, not just inhabit a
cell. That work should be as productive as possible, providing
an opportunity to learn work ethics and gain an education. With
today's technology we don't need to build so many multimillion-
dollar prisons to create security. Many prisoners who are clearly
not a threat to society's safety could be fitted with tracking devices
so authorities know where they are at all times without incarcer-
ating them.

In an ideal world prisoners would receive the kind of assistance they need during their internment, and I strongly believe we
need to encourage such procedures on a massive scale. It is simply
foolish to warehouse people and expect them to miraculously become worthwhile members of the community.

•

Fear is the antecedent of violence; ignorance is the antecedent of
fear. Only through communication can we achieve trust and gain
knowledge and get on the nonviolent road. In a world where few
people have the chance to work closely with the horse, we can
at least all share in the message I so firmly believe the horses are
telling us: violence is never the answer.

VIOLENCE THROUGH THE GENERATIONS

Parenting is one of the toughest jobs anyone can take on. It is also
the most important. To bring into the world balanced, loved and
loving people is what parents should strive for. We need to examine closely every area of child-rearing and be aware of all the messages, subtle or obvious, that we give our children. If the response
to my work as I travel the world has anything to teach me, it is
that people want to get violence out of their lives. Violence can
never produce a balanced person or a well-adjusted horse.

•

In the autumn of 1998 while doing demonstrations in the United States, I met two people whose story revealed the terrible legacy of abuse early in life. What they shared with me has recharged my efforts to assist families in crisis. I had "finished" the first two horses of a four-horse evening; that is, taken two raw, untrained horses through the Join-Up process in front of a large audience. I was in the middle of a half-hour intermission when I noticed a lady standing nearby. She appeared to be in her early forties and was slight of build. She had her arm round her daughter, who was about nine years old and looked as though she would closely resemble her mother one day. They were both shy and subdued. They didn't seem to be interested in advancing to get an autograph and remained distant, listening attentively to my question-and-answer session. I didn't give it much thought, but their image stuck with me.

I returned to my round pen and completed the session. The evening went very well and I came back to my signing stand pleased with the demonstrations. After twenty minutes or so I realized that the lady and her daughter were back in their original position. Once more, there was no attempt to come forward for a signature or to ask a question. On this particular night, I remained to talk to about twenty or so people who were interested in getting every piece of information they could.

It was obvious that the evening was winding down and I had already made a couple of moves to stand up. At this point the pair moved to the front of my stand. Both looked up at me with very passive body language and the lady said, "Thank you very much, Mr. Roberts, for all you are doing. You have changed my life."

"I have? How have I done that?"

"You have helped our family immensely. We have no horses

and I know nothing about them, but I have five daughters and you have helped so much with our family life."

"Thank you for telling me," I said. "I don't know about the other four, but that is certainly a pretty little girl you have there." With that the little girl ducked behind her mother and seemed to be very embarrassed. The woman looked up at me and her eyes glistened with moisture. "May I give you a hug, Mr. Roberts?" she asked. "Sure, step up here." I indicated the platform of my signing stand, and she stepped up. I stood up from my chair, put my arms out and gave her a big hug.

Suddenly I realized that she was in trouble. She grasped me as if I were a log in a flood-swollen river, and as it turns out, that is exactly what I was. She began to sob uncontrollably and all I could do was hold her and wait for the episode of extreme emotion to end. At one point I looked at the daughter and found that she was standing with her little hands pressed up under her chin and had rivulets of tears streaming down her face. I have had many people come to me with crises in the family, and I could immediately see that this fell squarely into that category.

The few remaining people began to drift away, reducing the embarrassment that the woman must have felt. Within a minute or two we were sitting on the edge of my signing stand, with the daughter standing just a few feet in front of us. I intended to give her a chance to be heard, and I was prepared for a horror story about how she had been beaten by a brutal husband.

"For four years," she began, "we home schooled our five daughters. I was pleased with the academic results we were achieving, but I simply got tired with all the shouting and hitting." She was still emotional and speaking through tears and sobs. "It finally came down to at least a beating a day and we decided that they would have to go to a normal school. That has been the case now for one year, but I believe we can now bring them back for home schooling again."

"What made the change?" I inquired.

"Well," she said, "my daughter who is standing here tonight checked a book out of the library and read it. It was your book *Shy Boy*. When she was finished with it, she brought it home for me to read. I was blown away. I saw in that book the reference to your first book, *The Man Who Listens to Horses*. I sent my daughter back to the library to check that one out. She did and by the time I was finished with it, I was overwhelmed by the realization of how wrong we have been with our daughters. We can now bring them home without any worry of physical abuse."

I must admit that I was a bit perplexed. "Did your husband read my books?" I asked. From past experiences I made the assumption that it had been the husband who had been abusive to the daughters. "No, he hasn't," she answered, "but it wasn't my husband who needed to read them." Now it was my turn to be blown away. I just couldn't believe that this slight, very feminine, young woman could engage in physical violence. "It was me," she confessed, "I couldn't help myself. Something clicks inside of me and I have to act out to try to control the situation. I always feel that I am doing it for the benefit of the child. Later, I hate myself and I wonder how I could act in this way."

"Were you abused as a child yourself?" I asked. "Oh yes," she replied, "I was beaten with regularity." She said she had often wondered when she was young if she would resort to such abuse herself. She said that she knew it was something she didn't want to do, but that it just happened. She hated every minute of it. Until she read my books, she indicated that she had absolutely no control over her urges to act out violently, but that she believed she could handle this demon now.

Once again I made an incorrect assumption. I asked if it was her father who had beaten her as a child. "No," she said, "it was my mother." She didn't believe that her mother ever felt any guilt for being violent with her or her siblings. She told me that her mother was beaten violently by *her* mother. Until then I think I hadn't recognized the degree to which women can be violent, too. This lady said to me that her maternal grandmother seemed to be quite a nice lady by the time she got to know her and had come to realize that she was responsible for a daughter who was out of control and extremely dysfunctional, because of violence. In the past she had pleaded with her daughter to seek counseling before she severely injured one of her granddaughters.

Her grandmother had broken bones and permanent scars from the beatings she had endured at the hands of her father. And when a man entered the scenario the cycle of violence intensified. Violence was a part of the lives of all the members of that family.

I offered to assist in setting up counseling and I explained that there was very little difference between her position and that of a recovering alcoholic or drug addict. She needed to deal with this one day at a time, to believe in the concepts and to stay the course, if at all possible. It is advisable to repent quickly and apologize if there is a reoccurrence of any sort, as well as express love and affection every day within the family group. It is just as important to set aside time when the family can talk and be close to one another as it is to produce the necessities of life such as meals. I recommended to her that she should try to speak freely to her daughters about the conflicts and tensions, and about the things that upset them, so that they might come to an understanding long before emotion came into play.

It's my solemn hope that my work with horses, and the demonstration evenings and books that come from it, will continue to help bring about the kind of catharsis this lady experienced. I, too, will stay the course, one day at a time.

A STORY

PB

Recently a horse that we will call PB was brought to Flag Is Up Farms. Unable to travel to see the horse, the owner had purchased it after watching a sales video, which can often be misleading. She had been impressed with the free jumping (an untrained horse being sent over jumps without a rider) depicted on the screen. When PB arrived at Flag Is Up he was taken, as a matter of routine, to the round pen after an appropriate settling-in period. Felipe Castro, who has worked for me since November 1980, was in charge of the "get acquainted" process that commenced. Shortly after beginning to work with PB, Felipe was severely kicked in the knee by what he described as the most volatile and dangerous horse he had ever seen.

In all his years at the farm Felipe has only once before been kicked or badly hurt, which is surprising because I have had him in every situation a horseman could imagine. Felipe was in the hospital when I heard about the incident, and I asked that PB be left out of training until I had a chance to work with him.

By the time I was ready to start training PB, Felipe was home in a cast and on crutches, able to describe for me a horse that was beautiful, athletic—but deadly. Felipe told me that PB could literally be standing quietly and then with no warning fly into a rage, kick at anything that moved and blast away from you at breakneck speed.

I entered the round pen and began to work with utmost caution. After Join-Up I carefully began to negotiate the procedures I normally use. Within fifteen or twenty minutes it seemed to me that PB was ready for the first saddle of his life. Aware of Felipe's warnings, I decided to use a surcingle as a first step in preparing PB. A surcingle is a beltlike object that has a girth much like a saddle, but not the weight or the bulk. It accustoms the horse to the feel of the girth. He was a bit spooky all right and tended to be on the flighty side, but I got the surcingle on him without great fanfare. I began to think that I was doing such a wonderful job that everything would just fall into place for the rest of the session. I moved him around the pen and he was a perfect gentleman, with no bucking or acting out.

I asked Felipe to bring the saddle into the pen while I was removing the surcingle and proceeded at once to put on first the pad and then the saddle. He accepted this and allowed me to straighten the girth on the off side (right side) with no resistance. I returned to his near side (left side), thinking how well I must be doing my work as he was cooperating without a complaint. I drew up the girth and dropped the tongue of the first buckle into a hole in the front billet. The next thing I knew PB's rear feet were clicked together well above my head. He kicked like no horse I have ever handled before; the bucking went on for several minutes longer than with any horse I had ever encountered.

Subsequent days of training brought me to the realization that PB had been whipped extensively, and almost every lash was on the near side. We were able to identify clear scars on his left hip, which precisely outlined the configuration of a chain. As I got to know him, I found that any quick movement along PB's left side would result in an immediate blasting away and kicking at anything that he felt he might reach with the hind foot. I spent a couple of hours each day with him and after five sessions I began to break through. Sometimes he refused to Join-Up, and I even had to get assistance to catch him in the pen. Remedial horses will often display unusual patterns. Although most raw, young horses will Join-Up solidly after two or three sessions, the remedial horse might have phobias so deep-seated he will be prone to a nervous skepticism for much longer. Finally I put a riding dummy on his back and he bucked so hard that he tore the head of the dummy right off.

The owner came to visit PB on the fifth session, and though he was maybe 30 percent as dangerous as on the first and second sessions, it was still pretty frightening to watch him in action. The owner looked me straight in the eye and said, "I'm not planning to take this horse home for me to ride and certainly not for my child, but I am concerned that he will never be safe enough even for the professional trainer that I have chosen for him."

The sixth session was a great improvement over the fifth and the seventh was equally as productive. I completed my eighth session with PB and was able to saddle, mount the dummy on him and long-line him (using two long reins, which allow you to walk behind the horse guiding him as if you were on his back) without one bucking jump. I could now make quick movements along his near side, which before sent him away from me at breakneck speed. Now he would stand quietly and even move a little closer to me. His Join-Up now manifested itself in a strong desire to be with me and he followed me everywhere I went in the round pen. There was absolutely no need to catch him—he caught me.

PB may well have faced humane euthanasia had I not met up with him, but now I believe that he will have a productive life as a professional show jumper. The reports we are now getting are that PB is training well and has demonstrated a great talent for show jumping. If PB is treated fairly, I believe that he will perform successfully, but if he experiences even the slightest taste of brutality he is very likely to return to his previous vicious state.

When PB came to me he had a truckload of emotional problems, which I call baggage. His past was obviously riddled with brutality. It took me time, but I was able to get him to check his baggage and put his fear and distrust on hold. Once I caused him to believe in me, we made great progress. I long for the day when all horses and people on this earth will be given a fair opportunity without force and demand.

Four
TRUST

Trust gives me my freedom and my
fear takes it away.
— JACK GIBB, *Trust*

WHAT WE ACHIEVE THROUGH JOIN-UP

The language of Equus is predictable, discernible and effective, as is the language of trust. In a trust-based relationship ground rules have to be established, and anyone who enters into one must take responsibility (the equivalent of the horse taking the saddle) for his actions. Any violation of the rules (such as bucking) must be dealt with in a nonviolent manner, which brings adrenaline down, in order to stay within my concepts.

Trust forms the basis of every moment of the process I use to start horses. Without trust, Join-Up cannot be achieved. Join-Up creates trust, which is pivotal to all good relationships and partnerships, whether between man and horse, employer and employee, teacher and student, parent and child or husband and wife.

The word trust comes from the German word *trost,* which

means comfort. Scandinavian in origin, it is similar to the word *treowe*, which is Old English for faithful. The parallel meaning of the two words is hardly surprising, as it is unlikely that you will be faithful to someone you can't trust.

Trust is created by many exchanges. It is stimulated by a shared interest, or an attraction to another person, because if you like someone, you want them to trust you and to share goals. Willingness and confidence inspire trust. It is also created through bonding experiences, through conversation or dependency: for example, the dependency of the baby on the mother.

Mutual bonding arises when two people trust each other and recognize each other's needs. In order to assess someone's needs, you have to ask questions and you have to listen—setting up such a conversation is paramount to the process of building trust. Join-Up is essentially a question-and-answer session in which each stage has to be completed before the conversation can continue. I ask, Do you want to stay out there or do you want to come in and Join-Up with my herd? It is only because I establish trust through this question-and-answer session that I can create a safety zone for the horse to enter, in which it feels comfortable enough to Join-Up with me. The reason I can saddle and place a rider on a horse in thirty or so minutes is only because I have developed a trust-based relationship. The horse views me as a trustworthy leader.

Fidelity is a quality that we look for in a friend; without trust it is difficult to maintain fidelity. The horse must therefore have faith in you as a leader, but if you inflict pain on a horse you will extinguish that trust. Many horses come to me bereft of faith due to the treatment they have received from handlers.

Children learn very quickly to protect themselves from attacks by adults. They are as much flight animals as are horses and will recoil or run from aggressive behavior, such as physical attacks or even verbal abuse. These negative experiences become the psychological baggage of the child. In order to dispose of them, someone must take the child through a new learning process, to reestablish trust and confidence and enable him or her to see adults in an acceptable light. If trust is not reestablished, an abused child is likely to grow into an angry and aggressive adult. Such children will often harbor resentment that is likely to express itself so that they become exactly what they detest. This environmental imprinting causes violence to travel through families, much like a dominant gene, so that it may for all the world appear to be an inherited trait as it was once generally believed to be.

Young, damaged adults are usually unable to talk through problems with family or friends and normally fail to communicate or negotiate well in the workplace, too. Some of them will mask their propensity for violence quite effectively, but they normally have a flashpoint where control is suddenly lost. Hence we often hear on the evening news, "Oh, he seemed like a quiet young man with no problems at all. I can't believe he did such a thing!" Others may express their violent tendencies openly and simply enter adulthood as aggressive bullies and social outcasts. Unless they can find someone to trust and someone who trusts them, these individuals are likely to contribute to our social ills.

I consider myself extremely lucky that the circumstances of my existence included horses, which gave me a safe zone, a place where I could go and find understanding and acceptance, away from my violent father. I suppose I might have found the same haven with dogs, cats, other animals or even other people. But it is my opinion that the horses are responsible for all that I am as an adult. I feel as though if I had not had the help of these animals I might have become a very violent man. During the 0–1 time frame of early childhood all human beings are imprinted significantly with their life's behavioral patterns, and unlike horses, humans have ego and often go to extraordinary lengths to hide their own aberrant behavior, to protect themselves from the detection of abnormal behavior. Horses are far easier to read because they have no reason to hide their emotion. They will tell you straight out. They have no ego and will communicate with utter honesty. People tend to mask their feelings of distrust so that they can gain trust from others, but the hidden factor will eventually surface to affect the relationship. Each horse that enters my round pen brings an arsenal of information about the human beings who have influenced him. Even the yearlings (horses under twenty-four months of age) tell me how they have been handled or dealt with in their short lives. I can quickly pick up from their responses their feelings regarding humans in general.

•

What about the corporate world? Do managers and executives fully understand the importance of trust? People are taken onboard in various positions within the corporate family. Why should a company bother to find out whether an individual trusts those around him or whether or not he trusts those responsible for him?

The enlightened executive knows that his company will only work efficiently when those within the framework of the team can justifiably trust one another. Ideally, individuals have been tested and earned the right to trust and be trusted. If company policy relies on a big stick rather than a big carrot it tends to erode trust. If the messages handed down to employees are confused or hard to discern, it equally erodes trust. The enlightened executive who identifies elements of distrust within his corporate family should take swift action to remove that influence from his team. It is critical in every organization to establish an environment whereby each employee is utterly confident that he or she will be treated in a fair and honest way when he or she achieves positive results. Likewise, every employee should face the consequence for negative behavior.

It is impossible to count the number of times that people have come to me saying things like "I can't believe what you do with horses. They frighten me to death. They are so big, I feel like they could kill me at the blink of an eye. How can you trust anything so large, flighty and unpredictable as the horse?"

Fear and mistrust can be delivered to you by two distinctly different messengers. First "the unfamiliar" and second "the familiar." Horses bring about fear in people generally because they are unfamiliar with them and have not taken the time to get to know that, although horses are large and fast, they normally have no desire to hurt anything. Fear of a parent, your spouse or your boss, on the other hand, might follow from the knowledge that they have a propensity to act violently.

I tell people who express great fear of horses to get to know them, to study their true patterns of behavior and to understand more clearly what the horses want out of life before branding them as dangerous. As I examine my own patterns of fear and distrust, it seems utterly foreign to think that I might fear a horse. Humankind, yes—but not horses, with which I am deeply familiar and which have never given me cause to distrust them.

If I could take all corporate executives and put them through a few sessions in the round pen with a horse, their understanding of trust would be elevated to such an extent that they would go back into the workplace with a whole new confidence. They would also assign more importance to what goes on in the lives of their colleagues, both inside and outside their workplace.

I have utilized this technique on many occasions and what I have found is consistently interesting and dramatic. The corporate officer unfamiliar with horses enters an environment that he is likely to find frightening. His pulse rate goes up and, uncertain of himself, he acts out in one of two ways. The assertive person will at once become overly aggressive and attempt to intimidate the horse and take charge of his surroundings. The less aggressive person will allow fear to drive him into a protective shell and he will often assume a very passive role as a result. Both responses have to do with how unfamiliar the new environment is and it is to be expected that they would have one of these two dramatic responses. I will talk the executive through a conversation with the horse so that together they can begin to work toward a better understanding of each other and accompish certain goals I have set out for them. It is amazing how two very different personality types that are poles apart will, when confronted with this large and hitherto frightening animal, both consistently work their way toward the middle ground and, with pulse rate down, come to an understanding of how to set up a relationship with the creature and successfully work with it to achieve common goals.

Once they gained a reasonable degree of familiarity with the concepts of Join-Up, it is my opinion that they would trust more, be trusted more and establish in themselves a degree of tolerance for the problems of their associates that would significantly improve their relationships both throughout the company and beyond.

It is essential that employers do their level best to understand both employees and potential employees as much as possible. They should become familiar with a man's ability to work with women if his job requires it, and the same is true for women working with men. When we put together a workforce we should know as much as possible about the individuals who make it up, and all things pertinent to their ability to perform.

A STORY

Blushing ET

*Do not complain about your neighbor until you have
walked a mile in his moccasins.*
—NATIVE AMERICAN SAYING

After the launch of my first book it became fashionable for segments of the media to present me with challenges that could then be filmed for release in various parts of the world.

Late in 1997 one such challenge came my way. It would eventually prove to be one of the most educational experiences of my career, requiring an approach more flexible than any I had known before.

Blushing ET was a racehorse whose career—and life—were to be ended unless he ceased his dangerous behavior at the starting gates. I was later told that it was thought the treatment he'd received before coming to me would make it an impossible task. I must say that Blushing ET tried hard to live up to that reputation and very nearly succeeded in defeating me. I sincerely believe that he meant no harm, but only acted out in an attempt to survive what he believed was a life-threatening situation. He had no faith in humans.

It was as though this particular horse sat back and said to me, "Until you get it right, I will be negative, angry and very dangerous. Even when you do get it right, I will be very careful to study it before I agree." He clearly demanded from me that I rework my usual thought patterns and migrate to his needs. I had to be innovative and willing to accept his time frame, holding to no established criteria.

When I began to work with Blushing ET I did Join-Up with him. Although he was skeptical, he joined-up well and it all looked hopeful. Then we took him to the starting gates, and that veneer of good behavior peeled away. He was terrified. People, even children, will reveal the character of their negative psychological baggage when closely observed. A child who has been abused will instinctively wince or duck if he or she thinks a well-aimed blow is on its way. That is the flight instinct in us. Many an abused child also develops aggressive tendencies as a defense. Similarly, an abused horse, when cornered, will reveal his underlying fear in a show of aggression.

When I first worked with Blushing ET, I could not perceive the extent or depth of his phobias. I knew that he was afraid of the starting gates and I knew it was the side rails in the starting gates that upset him (not a rare phenomenon with racing horses), but in the beginning I did not correctly and precisely assess his fears. He was an unusual horse in that, like a child, he effectively hid much from me.

People hide large portions of their learned behavior from other people in order to survive. They socialize when in fact they find it difficult to mix with people. They might be rather standoffish or even aggressive and unpleasant when deep down inside they are crying out to be loved and accepted. Perhaps they have been rejected so much by their parents or peers that they have learned like Blushing ET to be aggressively defensive. Attack is comprehensible when one considers that it is learned defensive behavior, whether among people or horses.

Rationally, there can be no justification for an offensive attack of any kind—whether on people, horses or countries—because violence is never the answer. To attack demonstrates an appalling inability to understand our own frustrations, inhibitions and fears and shows a refusal to deal with our own psychoses as well as an inability to communicate. Perhaps countries could develop a healthier philosophy to situations which threaten national security.

I worked with Blushing ET at the starting gates, attempting to get him to understand that they were safe and not a threat. Progress was slow, but there was progress nonetheless. After many weeks of constant work I took him to the Santa Anita racetrack where he demonstrated the extreme depth of his phobia.

Jay Slender, the head starter, and his crew were very helpful and cooperated as I introduced Blushing ET to racetrack conditions. I was allowed to handle Blushing ET myself in an effort to load him in the gate. Once he was in the gate I put a rider on him in order to simulate a race. I felt I had my equipment right and I asked Blushing ET simply to pass through an open gate for the first exercise of the morning. As I walked through the gate, Blushing ET suddenly went into a state of heightened awareness. He crouched down, trembling, with his eyes opened as wide as possible. He launched forward as fast as he could go, bashing into me as he passed through the stall itself. He ran to the end of my thirty-foot line and hit it like a freight train. I was able to stop his forward momentum and had to watch as he turned to come at me, striking out with his front feet.

Jay ran from behind the gate and helped me get control of the horse once more. After I knew everybody was safe, my knees went weak. I was trembling all over. Blushing ET was wearing a protective blanket across his hindquarters—a special kind of security blanket I had developed for horses terrified of the side rails in starting gates (now internationally known as the Monty Blanket)—and had Blushing ET got away from me, that blanket would have been very frightening to the fifty or more valuable racehorses then being worked out on the track. He would have been running uncontrolled around the one-mile track, dragging a thirty-foot nylon line and waving this frightening blanket behind him. I cringe when I think of what might have happened; my only comfort is that he had been handling the gate well when we left home, and his behavior at the track was a complete surprise.

Blushing ET caused me to realize that I had to deal directly with his deepest phobia—a fear of whips. What had started with his natural aversion to the starting gate had been compounded by trainers using whips to force him in. The harder they whipped him, the more he blamed the side rails—and every human who brought him near a starting gate. I found that I had been dealing with his fear response and not the root cause. He was trusting in other areas; he did not mind having bandages put on in the stable and was happy to be groomed, saddled and ridden around the track, but the instant he was presented with the starting gates he remembered what someone had done to him. This made him the most aggressive and dangerous horse you could imagine.

There is a Native American saying, "Do not complain about your neighbor until you have walked a mile in his moccasins." Blushing ET and I needed to find a way to understand and make allowances for the roads each of us had traveled. In doing so we can better understand the decisions people make, the company they choose and the expectations they have for their lives.

I was doing my best to "walk that mile" in Blushing ET's moccasins. I had to find a way to simulate the whips (without pain) around his hocks and cause him to think through his phobia and rationalize it. I also had to do it without being killed. Blushing ET proved to be deeply phobic about long lining, because the lines most closely resembled whips. I had thought at first that if I could get him to settle down in the starting gates through constant exposure under safe conditions, he would finally accept that it was a safe environment, but he showed little or no progress. Once I introduced him to the long lines, he wrestled with his fear as his memory of the pain rose up to dominate his actions. It became obvious that if I continued to work from the ground I might be killed as this massively powerful horse turned on me again and again. I wanted to help him so I had to discover some unique way to continue. As I worked with him one day, something told me that I could create a safe position for myself if I enlisted the assistance of my horse, Dually. I don't even know why, but I had already saddled Dually and left him in his stall before starting. I rode Dually into the round pen, and from his back I drove Blushing ET on the long lines. I allowed him to feel and express his fear, yet prevented him from doing any further harm to me. I can only surmise that Blushing ET felt animosity toward human beings, not toward horses. Humans had abused him with whips, not members of his own species. It is also true that I was mounted on a very fast and responsive horse that could maneuver me out of harm's way.

In order to touch the seat of Blushing ET's phobia I had to send him the information—daily in repeated doses—that the long lines were not going to hurt him, until I had truly desensitized him of his fear. This is not the first time that I have taken this route. Desensitizing is an important part of the work I do with horses facing a wide variety of problems. The cure is to repeat the simple message that whatever they fear will not hurt them. This has reinforced for me the importance of never using abuse and pain. I have seen too many horses sent to the killers because pain has been inflicted upon them.

I was able to drive Blushing ET in and out of the stalls repeatedly. Through the repetition of this exercise I was able to convince him that the lines were not whips, and that he could complete this maneuver and not come to harm. It took hours, but the result was obvious the next day when I repeated the process. We had finally broken the back of this phobic behavior and were on the home stretch. A few weeks later Blushing ET was returned to the racetrack, where he is now the proud winner of two races, both of international standards, one at Hollywood Park and the other at Del Mar. Now he has gone off to New York to continue his successful career.

Join-Up was the key to all the work I did with Blushing ET and we would finish every session with Join-Up to reestablish trust. The process of setting out basic rules of behavior by my methods may initially seem slow, but it is in fact both effective and fast. Force is neither of these things. As you utilize Join-Up, you begin to see it as a true tortoise and hare situation. Allowing the horse to choose his own course of action while making him responsible for his own decisions will very quickly set him on a positive track. If nonviolent discipline is necessary and is effected appropriately, the horse will very quickly choose to cooperate. Using the language of Equus allows you to negotiate a contract quite quickly, the basis of which is that the horse looks for positive reward for his positive actions. In the end, you will virtually always gain the desired results in a *far shorter period of time* than will the trainer who demands performance rather than requesting it.

Conflict was seeded in Blushing ET through man's inability to understand that saying "You must" is not an answer to anything. And unless we fully understand where a person or a horse is coming from and take him through simulated experiences that allow him to learn to trust, we cannot expect him to alter his behavior.

The horse will not attack unless its previous experience tells it that its survival is threatened. To a horse, a human may seem unpredictable, and therefore untrustworthy. All the work I do around horses is utterly predictable—the way I move, the quietness with which I work and the messages I give. It all follows a pattern. This behavior lets the horse know that I can be trusted. In building up this trust, I obtain the horse's cooperation and, more than that, I banish fear. Where there is fear, there is never true understanding or cooperation.

What is it that we need most of all in families and organizations? Cooperation, of course. Without cooperation at home, a family unit collapses. Without willing cooperation at work, production will go down and in some situations, as in a strike, cease altogether. When a horse balks at being loaded into a trailer, or bucks its rider off, it is refusing to cooperate with the goals of its rider or handler. You no longer share trust or a common aim, which is to work together. You have a mutiny on your hands.

Trust in any partnership is based around "I believe in you and I am prepared to go with you." As soon as you have proved to the animal that your judgment is inappropriate, you have opened the door to a breakdown of trust. If you have caused your horse pain or confusion, do not be surprised if he no longer trusts you. Why should any intelligent creature go down that path twice? Horses are far from stupid.

I do my best to have a trailer-loading problem at each of my demonstrations. I communicate with the horse and cause it to want to be with me. In his language I let him know that I mean him no harm. I ask him to step into the trailer and then once more using the language of Equus I cause him to understand that the trailer won't hurt him. I repeat the loading process eight or ten times as repetition is essential to any learning process. Most often they are obviously relieved when they are able to shed their phobia and accept the trailer willingly. Usually I am able to do ten minutes or so of communication and then literally load the horse easily within a matter of two or three minutes. These are horses that typically have been impossible to load for two or three years.

It is exactly the same with people. Abused people need much convincing before they are willing to trust again. Work has to be done to build up trust and care must be taken never to break it. They are no different from Blushing ET. Each asks the same question: "You hurt me once; will it happen again?"

Looking at the process of trust breaking enables us to find out more about the process of trust building. I allow people to make mistakes because they learn from their errors. Learning empirically is essential to achieving wisdom. But when do we draw the line? How many times can we sit and watch people make the same mistakes time and again before we act? It would be kinder to let them go and find something they are good at. These thoughts may well have been going through the head of a mule I once owned.

A STORY

Tina

Many of my experiences with animals have been memorable, and they have often served to demonstrate that, though we humans tend to believe that we are vastly more intelligent than the animals with whom we associate, sometimes we are wrong. The story I am about to relate to you happened in the early 1980s. What was dramatically humiliating about the event was that the animal involved was not some million-dollar purebred horse but a thought-to-be "lowly" mule (a cross between a female horse and a male donkey). Tina was not just any mule—she was a world champion—but a mule nonetheless. I am often asked about the intelligence of mules. My response is that the most intelligent horse you can find will almost always be one notch below the slowest thinking mule. Mules are a true hybrid and, in my opinion, have higher IQs than horses.

I had taken Tina to a 10,000-acre ranch about twenty miles from mine to assist a cattle roundup in the beautiful Santa Ynez Mountains. Dee, the foreman, paired up the riders and assigned them to various parts of the ranch.

"Monty," he said, "you go with Alvin and ride directly north up the center valley road. Go through the iron gate about three miles from these corrals. About a hundred yards after you have gone through the gate, the road will fork. Alvin, you take the left fork and Monty, you take the right. Each of you gather the cattle on the mesas [flat-topped hills divided by steep gorges or valleys] for the next two to three miles, right up to the north fence and then bring your cattle back down those same roads through the iron gate and on south to the holding corrals.

"When you have gathered all your cattle," Dee continued, "wait up on the mesas until both of you are prepared to descend the forks toward the iron gate. The cows have been sent to the branding corrals many times before and if one of you comes down off the mesas before the other is descending, they will do a U-turn at the bottom, refusing to go south through the iron gate. When you are both at the top of the forks and you can see each other across the canyon, then and only then send your cattle southerly down your respective roads."

Alvin and I struck out to the north. Alvin was on a beautiful gray quarter horse and I think he must have been chuckling under his breath at me, riding a brown mule with ears nearly as long as your arms. We rode for about forty-five minutes and then we saw the big iron pipe gate. I got off and chained it in the open position while Alvin held Tina. We rode on north for a few more minutes to where the primitive road forked, just as Dee had described. Each fork immediately began an ascent of about 800 feet within a mile or so to the huge mesas with a great gorge in between. Our task seemed elementary—to gather the cattle on those mesas and descend.

I was climbing northeast as Alvin was climbing northwest, and when I leveled out on the mesa, I could see Alvin as I looked westerly across the deep canyon. I waved and he returned it. Each of us went off to gather the cattle assigned to us. For the next hour and a half or so Tina performed as she always had, generously and without hesitation. I had about fifty or sixty cows with their calves at side when I arrived back at the point at which my road began its descent toward the iron gate. I circled my cattle and remembered the instructions Dee had given us; we were now in a holding pattern.

I had waited only about fifteen or twenty minutes when I saw Alvin appear on the mesa directly to the west of me. Once again I gave him a wave and I could have sworn I saw him wave back to me. Tina and I busied ourselves starting our cattle on their way. It was only another twenty minutes or so until I was at the convergence of the two roads. I realized that my cows and calves had made the U-turn and were starting up Alvin's road.

I couldn't imagine what had gone wrong, but I asked Tina to put it in high gear and run flat out up the road to head them off and bring them back down again. She did it like the champion she was and I was proud of her when I had gained control of the lead cow and turned them all back toward the iron gate.

You can imagine how I felt when I got to the bottom, only to discover that they had started back up my road. Once more I asked

Tina for extra effort and she gave her all. Again she took control of the cows and calves on my original road and we turned to descend once more. Where was Alvin? What had gone wrong? As I was riding back down it occurred to me that he must have lost control of his cows and had to go back out across the mesa in order to regather them. When I arrived at the bottom my cows once again started up Alvin's road. We had been doing so well I decided to ask Tina to take charge of the situation once more. But Tina did not just say, "No," she said, "Hell no!" It was as if she were saying to me, "You guys have crossed up your signals and you're asking me to play silly games here to cover up your mistakes. I am not going one foot up that road."

A few minutes later I could hear Alvin whistling at his cattle. He was bringing them down the mountain. I felt well rebuked by Tina's intelligent decision, and I admonished myself, realizing how stupid we human beings can be at times. I sat there on Tina as Alvin drove the cattle past me toward the iron gate. Thanks to Tina's decision to stay put, I was in a position to protect my fork and they had no other choice to make.

Tina never refused anything I asked of her before or since. It is humbling to realize that she trusted me to give her instructions that were productive, but when she tested the instructions and found them to be wanting, she suggested to me through her refusal that I should rethink the situation. She then proved to me that I had been trying to achieve my goal without considering whether or not it was fair to her. After all, she was doing almost all of the work; I was along for the ride.

•

There are many lessons to learn from this. For example, corporate executives focusing on the goals they wish to achieve sometimes overlook the obstacles—the canyons and the ridges—seeing only the final result. They issue orders and demand performance often without regard for the individuals who are responsible for completing the workload. They may be successful in achieving those goals, but if their demands are unreasonable, there will come a day when the hands-on doers dig their heels in and leave the executives wondering where they went wrong.

Repeated success is generally reserved for those employers who walk in the moccasins of their workers once in a while, so as to more fully understand the effort being put in. Employers should be logical with the workload request and see performers through to a successful conclusion, leaving them with sufficient energy to celebrate their performance when the final results are in.

Trust should flow through all walks of life. This higher level of cooperation can, if we embody these principles, improve the quality of our lives. Trust radiates out, extending the benefits of trust to the people around us, like ripples across a pond into which a stone has been thrown.

Humans think in extremely complicated patterns. We have phenomenal brains that we often put to work overtime. I admire those minds that can keep five balls in the air at once, but I have lived my life with simpler beings like the horse and spent time learning from them the basic elements of understanding. If we could only introduce these simple values to the most brilliant minds, we would create more balanced beings who could master the complex while appreciating the need for basic understanding. We would have an executive who not only possessed knowledge and creativity, but could tap into the wider understanding of the human spirit. These elements would, if brought together, create contentment in the corporate team.

Imagine, if you will, the sense of surprise that I experienced when I realized that I was being educated by a mule. I am a college graduate and a relatively intelligent human being, and many people consider the mule to be one of the simplest thinkers on earth. However, when I opened my mind and allowed myself to realize that we were in a partnership, I literally began to learn from her. Tina needed to trust me and conversely I needed to trust her. It was necessary for me to respect my partner in this project of ours and to acknowledge that, though she may be a simple thinker, she had her areas of expertise. I needed to trust her and respect the fact that her contributions could make the difference between success and failure.

I've learned to recognize the values in straightforward communication, through dealing with one of the simpler creatures on earth, Equus, a flight animal. I have been called a genius by well-meaning people who see value in the work that I do and are awestruck by how effective my methods are with what they perceive to be a wild and dangerous animal. It is fair enough to allow them that opinion, but it is, quite simply, the other way around.

•

Living with horses and dealing with their clearly defined set of rules and regulations is perhaps the easiest thing on my list of obligations. Since horses live with an absence of ego, not participating in such emotions as envy and greed, they are extremely predictable and they bring to the meeting no desire to harm or deceive. The human world has, by contrast, a deep history of unpredictability. Our son chose the law as a profession and specialized in business. What a fertile field this is in our litigious society where it seems to be considered normal for people to try to dodge their responsibilities. He currently manages our entire operation. The contracts, letters of intent and boilerplate agreements between my organization and other individuals are amazingly complex, a reflection of our world today.

Why do we need to create a mass of paperwork, complete with its demands and escape clauses? Because we don't trust. Why don't we trust? We don't trust because we have been lied to and cheated. We have too often dealt with people who came to the relationship with the intention of taking advantage. It doesn't matter whether it is countries, companies or a fifteen-year-old daughter. The outcome is nearly always the same. Confrontation, be it a war or a family argument, is most likely spawned from a feeling of mistrust.

In my experience mistrust between people finds its beginnings in the acceptance of violence, whether physical or verbal, as a solution to problems. Jack Gibb, author of *Trust*, suggests that if the world would at once concentrate on educating society through a far greater emphasis on eliminating violence and enhancing trust in the areas of major institutions in government, education, science and business, the world would take on enhanced tranquillity in a very short order. This enhanced tranquillity has its greatest potential now. Now is the time when the powers and superpowers of history can break the fever of conflict that has plagued our history.

In the round pen I have to create enough trust within the horse to override the natural fear factor that ordinarily puts him to flight. If I can communicate clearly enough with him, to convince him that his safety has a better chance with me than away from me, I have a chance of success. Remember that the deep-seated fear of a strange object on the horse's back is the result of "survival of the fittest," which has shaped the animals' behavior for approximately fifty million years. The following is an observation that I might have written word for word after starting many thousands of horses.

"Trust gives me my freedom, fear takes it away." Jack Gibb lays out, in a few words, the essence of why young people need a safe haven and people they can trust. "Trust is . . . trusting life."

Let us take a moment to reflect that for centuries man has made one curt demand of the horse: perform or face physical punishment. The person making this demand is often actually fearful of the harm the horse could do to him.

Every horse enters the round pen in a state of fear—that is the very nature of this animal. When both horse and man operate on the basis of fear, danger is ever present. One thing horses have taught me is that fear begets fear. If I create an environment that causes the horse to fear me, then he will probably act in a manner to cause me to fear him. A fear-based response will create a vicious circle of negative behavior. If man is to eliminate his fear of this large, athletic and flighty beast, he must learn to communicate in that creature's own language.

When adrenaline levels are up, learning is down, and when adrenaline levels are down, learning is up. The teacher or the parent who operates on the basis of fear, without trust, may create a young person who salutes and marches, but who falls short of reaching his or her full potential.

A CORPORATE EXPERIENCE

CSX and Tropicana

Since 1986, managers and executives of corporations from all over North America have been coming to Flag Is Up Farms to watch me work with raw, green horses in the round pen. The companies that send them, from IBM to Ford, are obviously convinced that there is merit in witnessing in person the Join-Up process.

Anyone who has seen the gentling of a horse often reports being moved by the sight of a powerful flight animal working past fear to indecision and finally to trust. The moment of Join-Up, when the horse delicately touches my shoulder with his muzzle, often elicits a gasp of wonder and delight from the audience.

A little horse sense would go a long way in the workplace. But the gap is often wide between bosses and workers, between CEOs and those below them in the corporate hierarchy. Traditional horsemanship has been based on fear for thousands of years; the workplace has long deployed the same tactics.

From personal experience I can tell you that change—certainly in the horse world—is hard and slow. But the message of the round pen is a powerful one, and in my own lifetime I have seen the world of horses transformed radically. Tens of thousands of horse people around the globe have embraced the principle of "request," rather than "demand." Wouldn't it be wonderful if a like number of corporate CEOs could come to the farm, work with a horse and return to their offices, sharing these principles with others?

There is growing evidence that watching me communicate with horses has had an impact; no longer am I alone in thinking the way I do. The workplace may indeed be ready for change.

Tropicana Products Inc., the major producer of fruit juices, and CSX Transportation Corporation, the rail-shipping giant contracted to move all that juice, were both well-established firms. Both treated their employees much like traditional horsemen treated their horses. Both companies were struggling with their relationship with one another; in fact, both felt as though they were at war with each other.

Keen to improve Tropicana's performance, the senior management called in Foxworthy Consulting, of Virginia. It so happens that Bob Foxworthy and I had by this time joined forces. He has been a corporate consultant for decades and has developed a system he calls "trust-based leadership." His work closely parallels mine and we occasionally put on corporate symposiums called "Trust-Based Join-Up." Our two philosophies fit like a glove.

With Tropicana, Bob faced a seemingly impossible task. In order to effectively compete in the global marketplace, Tropicana laid out a three-year set of goals that had to be met—or else. Tropicana managers went into a fear mode. They told the owner that the first year might be met if enough pressure was applied, but the second was highly improbable and the third utterly impossible.

Bob Foxworthy and his team went into action. Modifying behavior, he said, comes down to the individual. How we treat each other at work determines whether that company succeeds or fails. The positive environment begins on the shop floor and reflects up to and down from management, just as my treatment of a horse as an equal and respected partner creates optimal performance in the saddle.

Bob knew, as I do, that trust displaces fear. After huddling with many managers in many different locations within Tropicana, Bob was convinced that at heart his task was a basic one: eliminate fear and its causes and change the corporate culture that supported and protected the right to demand and force, as opposed to allow and ask.

His team began by working in two Tropicana departments. Bob called them "the trim tab" leaders. In the world of high seas shipping, the trim tab is a small rudder set into the larger rudder of a tanker. The ship is so large that the rudder itself will not turn without the help of this smaller one, which is only 5 percent the size of the main rudder. It's a tidy metaphor: you only need to enthuse 5 percent of the employees to create change within the company.

When productivity in the two departments took off, a third section showed interest and finally the entire company. Over a three-year period, Tropicana improved its productivity, enjoying a 150 percent return on its investment. Trust-based leadership was working. And when Pepsi bought the firm, it continued the process.

At one point Bob had met Gene Zvolensky, then Tropicana's director of distribution and now vice president.

"What is the worst problem you have at the moment in Tropicana?" Bob had asked.

Gene replied without hesitation, "We do have a problem. It's our relationship with CSX."

CSX Transportation had been a railroad company for 175

years; its management practices seemed rooted in the nineteenth century. Theirs was a fear-based corporate culture. But because CSX was responsible for moving so much of Tropicana's product, Tropicana's performance was tied directly to that of CSX. And the working relationship of these two companies was tense and hostile, like two predators glaring at each other for a share of the same piece of meat.

Bob tells the story of CSX workers inspecting the train one burning hot Florida day while Tropicana supervisors drove around the work site in covered, air-cooled golf carts. The men in the carts hurled taunts and obscenities at the workers. That moment seemed to symbolize the animosity between the two corporations.

But while Bob Foxworthy was working with Tropicana, it appears that CSX executives were looking on with great interest. On their own they had concluded that they had to change the old system that many employees were now resisting. When Tropicana volunteered to arrange a meeting between the two firms, Bob said it was like watching two porcupines mate.

Foxworthy's team introduced "trust-based partnership" to CSX, knowing full well that it had to start at the top and that these two companies needed to communicate. A pilot project gathered about twenty-five well-chosen people from each company, including union members and supervisors. They gave themselves four months to test the viability of a trust-based environment.

The Tropicana people could speak firsthand about how the new system encouraged innovation and feedback. They had learned the value of respecting one another and communicating in a civilized fashion. Foxworthy had employees shaking hands each morning and starting their days with cordial communication. He had executives inquiring about the personal needs of employees right down the line. It wasn't long until change was being noticed at CSX. A good apple in the corporate barrel can clear out the rot.

Both companies improved their performances as processes of congratulation, recognition for improved productivity and tools to improve the personal and emotional lives of employees were put into place. One good thing led to another. On-time deliveries broke records. Totals of juice delivered skyrocketed, resulting in soaring profits. Employees contributed ideas that made a difference. Everybody rose on the same tide.

At the end of the four months, Gene Zvolensky of Tropicana spoke at a general meeting of all participants. His words were aimed at his CSX colleagues. "We've been doing business with you for twenty-eight years," he said. "And in the last four months we've actually been partners."

After the trial period, the successful partnership continued. Recently, the two firms received two awards, including one from the Innovation Network, an American organization that encourages innovation in the corporate world.

A STORY

Betrayal

There are many things that have surprised me since 1989 when the queen of England viewed and endorsed my work. Amazement on the faces of those I considered to be good horsemen was a surprise to me. The number of books sold and the overall interest in my work was astonishing. The overwhelming factors are too numerous to recount.

Above all, the responsibility I feel toward the people I have touched so deeply has been sobering. I simply did not know that watching a horse being trained could bring forth the emotions that I see at virtually every demonstration. I suppose there is something to be said for the fact that nearly every one of us instinctively realizes that the horse cannot lie. When we witness a horse bond with and trust a human being we instinctively identify with this vulnerable flight animal forming a partnership with a predator. Victims of abuse who see this expression of mutual respect between horse and human must wonder what their lives would have been like in a safe environment.

I suppose there was some feeling deep inside me that suggested that I was the only one who understood the indescribable connection between a fight animal and a flight animal. Little did I know that a significant percentage of our society understands it full well. It may be a subliminal understanding, but an understanding nonetheless. I've yet to conduct an event where no person approached me after the demonstration. At least one audience member comes to me ready to bare his soul, breaking down and sharing with me some of the most emotional and deeply scarring stories you can imagine.

The power of communication must never be underestimated. We hear of trauma hidden in people's psyches, the result of emotional scars so deep they can never be erased. People who survive wars, natural disasters, plane crashes and the like often bond as a result of the experience. The trauma may dissipate, but the scars will always remain.

The story I am about to tell you is one that profoundly affected me when I heard it, and indeed ever since. I did not write down the name of the woman in question. I have attempted to locate her without success. There have been many times when I have thought that her story must be a nightmare, as it seems no one could have endured the kind of torture that she went through. But as I sat there and listened to her, I was mesmerized by the ring of honesty that I heard in every word.

Then there was the question, does it belong in this book at all and if so, why? The crimes perpetrated in this story are horrendous— where is the lesson in this? These are contemporary acts perpetrated in the twentieth century, acts designed to control and use others without the slightest regard for the victims. I ask myself if these same crimes are being perpetrated elsewhere and by others today and the answer is yes. This story begs to be included in this book because it reveals a common pattern of abuse and control— one that I hear about a great deal when doing my demonstrations, from the men and women who wait after the events to speak with me. Her story in particular tells of the most fundamental betrayal of trust—that between a parent and a child.

I was on tour doing a demonstration at an equestrian center when a lady approached me and asked me to sign several books. She had graying hair and a kind face with a smile that made you feel warm all over. As she began to talk, I realized that the next lady in line was actually with her. I was at once impressed by the demeanor of this second lady, who was probably in her late thirties. It was very clear that she had been pretty in her youth. She was one of those women fortunate to be blessed with jet black hair and milky smooth skin. Although she had lines below her cheek bones and wrinkles at the corners of her eyes that told of times of anxiety, her true beauty shone through.

The older woman told me that her friend had read my book and had been asking if there was any way that she could speak with me, or better still, meet me in person. She indicated to me that it was very important for her young friend to share her story with me. Many people come to me with similar requests, and as you can imagine, it is sadly impossible to deal with all of them on a personal basis. In this particular case, however, I felt compelled to respond. I took her aside and we sat down together.

I was to become familiar with a human tragedy the likes of which I had never known before. In an attempt to do her story justice, I am relaying it in her voice and in the spirit of her words as I remember them.

I was born an only child to relatively poor parents, and when I was in the early grades of grammar school, about the age of nine, I noticed that my mother would become a different person in the evening. She got really loud, cussed at my father a lot, threw things around and complained about not having enough money. This would go on for a couple of hours and then she would suddenly be asleep on her bed. I would prepare myself for bed on my own.

I came to the realization that my mother changed dramatically after having several drinks from bottles she kept high in the cupboard. She would try to drink from these bottles without my father or me noticing, while my father would openly drag bottle after bottle of beer from the refrigerator and sit in front of the television set, drinking them and throwing the empty bottles down beside his chair. He would often have me get the bottles for him and open them. I learned to do this at a very early age.

I asked him why he drank so much of this stuff and what it did for him. He told me that it relaxed him and said he had to have a few of these bottles each night to put up with my mother's anger. One night he asked me to bring him a beer and when I arrived beside his chair he was sitting with his bathrobe open down the front. I knew nothing of male anatomy and it was a shocking sight to me, but I couldn't help but look at all this humanity with strong curiosity. He seemed to be asleep, but I suddenly realized that he had opened his eyes and had been watching me. He asked me if I would like to touch him. I was frightened. It seemed ugly and repulsive and I dashed straight to my bedroom.

We lived in a very small house and I had a very tiny room. My mother was asleep (or passed out) and her door was wide open. As I curled up in bed, my heart was pounding with a fear that I hadn't known before. I didn't even know why I was frightened, it just seemed to sweep over me. There was a shadow at my door. I looked up to see my father standing just inside my room. I quickly noticed that his robe was hanging open and he was fully exposed. I closed my eyes and curled even tighter in a little ball. I heard him say that it was time that I learned a little more about what made men men and women women. He was then standing over me.

I felt him take hold of my arm and pull my hand toward him. He was pressing my hand in places I knew it shouldn't be. I yelled no to him and then I felt an extremely strong hand squeeze my shoulder as he admonished me to be quiet or I would awaken my mother. He then knelt beside my bed and buried me with his huge upper body. He said he loved me and that I'd made him very happy by touching him. He told me that my mother refused to touch him any more and that men needed this or they would go crazy, and that my mother was an alcoholic.

I felt fear, pity and obligation all rolled into one. I sincerely believed that my father needed my help and this time as he pushed my hand to him I realized that his anatomy had changed. He was gasping and I was certain he was dying. Once more I was terrified, as he fell on top of me. He then said wonderful things to me about how great I was and how much he loved me. I was very confused.

I remember vividly wanting to tell somebody about what had happened. My teacher came to mind, but he was a man and I was frightened to discuss this with him. The preacher at the church where we went every Sunday morning was a man I thought I could trust, but he seemed very friendly with my father. I knew I could never tell my mother who had by this time become very mean to me. I worked hard to help with the housecleaning, doing the dishes and all that sort of thing, but my mother was never happy with anything I did. She often took me by the shoulders, shook me and then slapped me across the face, saying I was lazy and too slow with my work. She would often hit me as punishment for something I hadn't done. I was pleased when she would go to her room with a bottle. It meant that the day was over for her and I wouldn't be the target of any more of her rage.

After that first night with my father, he began to protect me from my mother. He would stop her from hitting me and they would fight, ending up with her taking a bottle and going to her room. I began to view him as a protector, but my only real comfort lay in playing with my dog, Red, or Mouser, the stray cat that inhabited the dark space under the back porch. I took every opportunity to spend time with them. I loved my animals. They were good to me. They never hurt me and they always seemed to be my friends.

When it got dark my father would yell for me to come in the house. My mother's door would be closed and he would instruct me on things to do with him, which would cause him to gasp. I learned over the next six to eight months that as soon as he gasped, he became a nice man. He said nice things to me and then he went away and left me alone. I became quite willing to help him gasp so that it would be over.

It was my tenth birthday, and a Sunday. My mother made me a cake and it had ten candles on it. It was a lot of fun because everyone laughed as I was trying to blow them out. There were about five of my father's friends there and soon after the party my mother retired to her room. My father sent his friends away and told me several times that he had a special birthday present for me— I was to receive his body somehow inside of me. I clearly recall his awful attempts and the excruciating pain. I screamed and my father ran out of the room when I heard my mother's voice. I was really frightened, but nothing happened and everything got quiet. When I woke up in the morning, I found that my sheets, nightgown and legs were covered with blood. As quick as I could I was at the washing machine trying to wash away the evidence.

My mother saw the sheets and I stood in abject fear as she said to me, "Oh, don't worry about that; it will happen once a month from now on." I believed that she knew what my father had done and I was certain that it was planned that he do this once a month from that day forward. I got closer to my animals and tried to stay out of the house as much as possible while waiting out that month.

When my father approached me at night, I would very quickly take hold of him and give him satisfaction as rapidly as I could to protect myself from the next attack. The next few months went by and the attack didn't occur and there was no blood. I didn't mention a word about it to my mother, but she gave me some cotton pads with an elastic belt and she showed me how to put it on and said when the blood came again I was to use these. I was certain that she meant when my father attacked me again, but I was so confused I didn't dare ask for an explanation.

I was nearly eleven when one night my father was very drunk with one other friend. I went to bed and in a few minutes I realized that his friend was in the room with me. I pretended to be asleep and the friend pulled my arm, putting my hand to him like my father. I ran straight to my father and told him that the man came into my room. He held me close and whispered in my ear that his friend's wife wouldn't touch him either and that he too needed my help. I tried to say no, but it just wasn't going to work. I went back to my room; I caused the friend to gasp. I went to sleep and another night went by.

During the next months my father sent many of his friends to my room. I didn't fight it. I knew what to do, and I did it as quickly as possible. As long as they didn't try to hurt me, I went along with them. A couple of his friends began to do that other thing. I would bite and scratch them and run out of the room. My father promised that he would tell them never to do that again. I looked upon him as my protector.

I was twelve years old when I noticed that I was beginning to push on my shirt a bit from the inside. One night I realized that the blood was coming again, but no one had hurt me. By this time some school mates had helped me to understand a little more about what was going on. I wore my pads and asked my mother for more when I needed them. She never enquired about the three-year absence of the need for any of the pads.

One day I was in school and my teacher asked me to stay after class, saying that I needed special help. He took me to a room that was very dark and quiet and told me that he had heard that I knew what to do with men. I said I would help him gasp if that is what he wanted, but he was insistent that he do this other painful thing. I screamed, but there seemed to be nobody around. This time I was violated in every way. I was sure I needed to kill myself as life was just not worth living. I went to the girls' room and stuffed my underclothes with paper hand towels.

Some of my classmates had told me about social workers who came to school who would help if we had any trouble. I ran to find this social worker, who took me in and listened to me in a way I had never known before. She seemed kind and understanding and took me at once to the police department, where a police lady and the social worker escorted me to a nearby clinic.

I was put on a small bed with very white sheets. There were hoops over the bed so that the sheets were off my body. There was a nurse on either side and a lady doctor came in to examine me. The lady doctor spoke to me in a very gentle tone and I was comfortable for the first time in several hours. She told me that I was right to come to them and that no matter what anybody told me it is always best to seek help if someone has violated you. We returned to the police station and I was very frightened again. I saw my parents there and my mother seemed extremely angry, but my father put his arm around me. I learned about a month later that the teacher had lost his job and had moved away. I returned to school about a week after the incident and we now had a lady teacher.

I spent the next several months cooperating with the group of older males that had become regulars around our house and mother continued her drinking and passing out. I found that a pony had moved in about half a mile from our house. He lived on a vacant lot that had been fenced. I didn't know who owned him, but it didn't matter. The owners didn't seem to be around very much and the pony and I developed a close relationship. Along with my dog and cat, they became my best friends.

I told my father that we had to stop doing these terrible things because it just wasn't right and I might have to talk to my social worker. He explained that if I told anybody about what was going on, the family would be broken up. My father suggested that, instead of the social worker, he would bring the preacher from the church, who would make me understand that I had been born with a special gift of beauty that stirred men to their very core. A female social worker would never understand this as they don't often work with young girls with this special gift. I believed him, not that I was happy about it, but there was no question that I could now see that I was beautiful and it pleased me to be special.

The preacher came and he discussed with me all of these things that my father had said. He was very rough with me and he did the same thing as the teacher, only he went slower and I didn't bleed. It took him a long time to gasp and I began to hate the sight of him.

He came in one Sunday evening, when mother was already well under the influence. Soon she went off to her room. The preacher took me into the bedroom. Maybe he had been drinking, too, but he was very harsh with me and he told me that I would burn in hell if I didn't do exactly what he said. I resisted this force and he hit me several times right across the face. I ran from the house sobbing. The next thing I knew I was in the field with the pony, lying in the high grass where the men could not see me. I watched them drive by several times looking for me and under the protection of darkness I ran to the house of my social worker. She told me that if I was ever in real trouble I could come there.

She took me in and put ice packs on two badly swollen eyes. She called the clinic and a nurse came by in five minutes or so, examined me and took a statement. I had clawed the preacher man as hard as I could and the nurse cleaned under my nails and had me give her my panties. She placed them into a little plastic bag.

I spilled the whole story to them. I told them everything that had happened for the past three years. They took me to a clinic where I had a chance to bathe and they admitted me for further observation. The social worker spent the night with me there and I cried the whole time. My family was gone now. My father would be insane; I didn't have a home and I wouldn't even see my animals again. The following morning I was taken to a room in the county court building.

My mother, father and the preacher were there, as well as a judge of the family court system. The judge asked if he could see me in private and my social worker requested that she be present. The two of them took me to another room and I told the judge the whole story, just as I had told my social worker before. The judge said to me that he was a very close friend of the preacher, belonging to the same church, and while the preacher had made a mistake, he really believed that he was only trying to help me. The judge said, "You see, with that full chest of yours, the jet black hair and those beautiful eyes, you are a walking problem for all the men around here."

My social worker was uneasy with this and said that I shouldn't have to apologize for my looks, but the judge decided that this was a family problem which could best be worked out by the family. He committed me and my parents to an honor farm for a ninety-day period. The preacher would be there, too, and it would be explained to the preacher's family that he was there as an adviser. My mother and father were to stay off alcohol during this ninety-day period, and a psychologist would check us about three times a week to monitor the progress. The four of us would work it out on our own and at the end of ninety days he would reassess the situation. In the meantime I would remain at the clinic for observation and have psychological therapy designed to teach me to live without tempting men.

That night in the clinic I found myself all alone in a large kitchen area. I went to an area near the stoves where there was a large wooden cutting block with big knives in a slot on the side. I was sobbing by this time, as I knew what I had to do. I took one of the knives out of the slot and pressed it to an area in front of my left ear then pulling it across my face just below my cheek bone and toward my upper lip. I remember the blood gushing down onto my white robe. It shocked me into consciousness and I threw the knife across the room.

Only seconds later, two nurses came bursting into the kitchen, apparently having heard the bang of the knife. I was sobbing uncontrollably as they swept me up in their arms and took me down the hall. They belted me onto a gurney and the next thing I knew I woke up in my room with bandages all round my face.

My social worker was there and I recall the first words I said to her were, "I'm not pretty anymore so they can leave me alone now. I'm going to be ugly." She was crying now. She said that she would do what she could to keep me from going to that honor farm with my parents and the preacher. By the time my week was up, I found that my first day at the honor farm had been put

off for one more week until the stitches were removed. I
also learned that my social worker had been fired. I had a
new social worker assigned to me.

They came to get me on a Monday morning and I
was taken in a bus with four male prisoners to the honor
farm. I tried not to look at any of them, but I really did
want to know if they were turned off by my scars. I had
seen them in the mirror and I must say they were not
nearly as ugly as I hoped they would be. When we arrived at the honor farm I was shown to a three-bedroom
bungalow, which they said I would share with my parents and the preacher.

There was no therapy at the farm and no intention
on the part of anyone to change. There were people coming and going all the time. My parents had already made
arrangements for alcohol to be available. The preacher
said he apologized for being so harsh with me, promising
that he would be more considerate.

The first night on that honor farm was the same as it
had been at my own home. My mother was drunk by
dark and before ten or eleven o'clock I had caused each
of the men to gasp and they were sleeping. I went outside
but there were guards who refused to allow me to walk
around to see the animals on the farm. They physically
shoved me back into the house and told me to go to bed
or they would arrange to have me locked up.

As the bus had brought me in that afternoon, I had
looked the property over very closely. It might have
been an honor farm, but for all the world it was in fact a
pig farm with hundreds of hogs in large fields. The following night, the men settled down and went to sleep
early. Mother was in a stupor and I slipped down to the
back door with an armload of clothes and a jacket all

rolled up in which I hid salami and cheese. It seemed to me I had enough food for two months.

I crossed three rows of fences and picked a field with a few pine trees for extra cover. Out in these fields were little huts made of metal, which came right up out of the ground and made a half-circle dome shape about forty feet long and open at both ends—they were about half my height at the tallest point. They were intended to give the pigs shade and a cool place to wallow. If I were to go into the center of one of these buildings, nobody could see me there. As I approached my chosen hut, the pigs moved away from me but didn't set up too much fuss.

The opening to the building was very small, which meant that people were much less apt to find me in there. What I didn't bargain on is that heavy rainfall creates a lot of moisture and the pigs root up the ground to make a pudding of the soil. It becomes a tacky mud about ten inches deep, and as the sun doesn't reach inside these shelters they remain a wallow all the time. The smell was wretched, but I supposed I could get used to that. I got to the center and stretched myself back against one wall. I was prone now with some of the dryer mud as a pillow. Several pigs came in and took up residence near me, and then I slept long and hard.

I opened my eyes to realize that the world was bathed in bright sunlight. I could see that there was a truck out in the field, which had dumped its contents out the back and onto the ground. My roommates were all running out toward the truck as if Santa Claus had arrived—it was refuse, which was being dumped as part of the pig-feeding program. It was then that I heard a siren, and I knew that my parents or the preacher had awakened to discover that I was no longer in the house.

The guards began to show up like ants on the roadways. They had shotguns and were yelling my name. I heard sirens going around the perimeter fence outside the farm and I felt a bolt of terrible fear go through me. What would they do with me when they caught me? I watched them looking into the huts in the fields closer to the houses and I knew that sort of search would take place right where I was. I felt a surge of freedom that I had never known before. I didn't want to be found and I didn't want to turn myself in. The pigs were coming back to my hut now and I pressed myself deeply into the soil.

It was probably half an hour or so before I heard the voices of two of the guards. It is hard for me to look back and believe what I did at that point, but it seemed an easy decision to make. I pushed against the wall and the dryer soil next to it and slithered into this soup, between two agreeable pigs. While I could breathe, I was virtually entirely submerged and I felt safe. I was warm enough and I can recall the comfort I felt with the animals. I began to believe that the pigs were trying to protect me.

It was then that I heard a guard right at the end of my metal hut. He must have been on his knees, looking in and he banged some object on the top of it and yelled out, frightening the pigs. It really did scare the pigs and me, too. All the pigs let out grunting sounds and they leapt to their feet, some darting out at the far end of the hut. Whether it was a conscious effort or not, the two pigs on either side of me simply lifted themselves nearly to their feet and then settled back down again and I heard the man walking away.

That day I came to the conclusion that I could literally live there, and that I was being protected. I had food that was being delivered each day by these trucks, and the water devices placed throughout the field for the pigs were just fine for me.

By this time my jeans, my light blue top, face, arms and everything about me was black, painted with the muck that was my protector. I became as stealthy as any cat burglar and I found myself able to visit some of the buildings and go on walks. There were several close calls, but I learned very quickly how to use the pig wallows in the field to be out of sight in the blink of an eye. It was on one of these evening jaunts that I met an eleven-year-old boy from a family that lived just outside the prison fence. My friend told me, about two weeks after I met him, that the prison guards had come to the conclusion that I was outside, but that some official from the city wanted a clean sweep of the honor farm with bloodhounds, just to eliminate the possibility that I was still there.

The next day I heard the bloodcurdling bays of the pack of bloodhounds. I was certain that this would spell the end. The pigs were quite nervous about the blood-hounds and at first they circled the field with their tails held high. As the awful sound of the hounds came closer and closer, they needed the protection of the hut. They descended on me with speed and charged into the build-ing with a purpose I had not witnessed before. They hud-dled close to me and I felt they were intent on hiding me. I was buried in the muck in the center of the building, and not one animal stepped on me or even banged into me. Suddenly I realized that two very large pigs were ly-ing one on each side of me.

They were particular favorites of mine, and as far as I was concerned, they knew quite well what they were do-ing and why they were doing it. As the hounds de-scended upon us, the pigs moved tighter and tighter against me. The hounds were right outside the hut now and the fear within me was at the highest possible level. I thought they would catch scent of me, come directly to me and signal exactly where I was with their baying.

The pungent odor of the hogs probably completely overwhelmed the senses of the hounds and they were unable to identify me. One hound slipped into the hut along the wall, stopped right in front of me and looked at me. He just stared for a couple of seconds and my heart seemed to stop. Then he quietly left the building. I heard the men cursing and the wail of the dogs growing fainter as they moved on to another field.

For the next few weeks I met more often with my friend at the fence. By this time the muck that covered me was caked dry in thick layers, and while I considered it my friend and protector, my skin was beginning to break out in sores. I know now that I was suffering from skin fungus virtually all over my body.

The boy said that there was a confidential crisis counselor at his school. He worked it out so that she met me at the back fence. She knew the social worker who had befriended me and she brought her along. When the two of them saw me they burst into tears. They promised me that they would arrange to protect me from all of the things that had violated me in the past. They said that they would be back at that spot in the fence the following evening and I was to meet them there.

I spent the last night there overwhelmed with the bittersweet thought of leaving my pigs. I was in fact a part of their family. I hugged each one of them and they seemed to know and understand that I needed help. To this day they are, at least in my mind, my friends.

At the agreed upon time a car, a truck and an ambulance appeared at that back fence. My two social workers were in the first car, as well as two men in suits and ties. Four men got out of the truck—they were uniformed officers with guns and billy clubs. I was very frightened. I remember saying, "Please don't hurt me, I really didn't do anything wrong."

I kept repeating to the ladies, "Don't leave me alone." There was a lot of light in the ambulance. It had been a long time since I had been in the presence of such brightness, as during the daytime I stayed in the center of my hut. It dawned on me, realizing that I could now be seen so clearly that I should ask the two ladies, "Am I ugly now?" I repeated several times, "I want to be ugly. I think I must be ugly now."

I was kept in a medical facility, and while they were careful to provide me with female attendants who were understanding and reassuring, I went through some incredibly tough times for the next thirty days or so and many times I wished I was dead.

•

I listened amazed and horrified to her tale. As if she felt she needed to give me proof, she rolled up her sleeves and showed me the scars on her wrists, the results of several slashings. I quizzed her as to how serious she was about killing herself. She indicated that she really didn't want to die, but on the other hand she did not want to face life as she had come to know it.

When the older lady joined us she explained to me that her younger friend was now living on an animal rescue farm. She had an apartment above the barn and spent all of her time working with neglected and abused horses that had come to reside there. I suppose that this should give each of us cause to stop and wonder how this species of ours could come to be so cruel.

Five

RESPECT

My word is my bond.

A STORY

Brownie

Toward the end of 1948, I acquired a very good horse called Brownie, but I had a problem with him that I now know is very common in the training of competition horses. He taught me a lesson—one with wide implications for families and businesses—about the damage we do by making unreasonable demands, whether there are too many of them or the individual demands are excessive.

When I look back I realize how much more effective a horse he could have been with a more accomplished trainer. By the age of thirteen I had already won many championships and was a highly trained performer in the Western Division, but in retrospect I am able to see many areas where I was incompetent. Brownie helped me to understand that sometimes it is necessary to know when to take the pressure off. As Brownie's "employer" I was demanding

Right: A talk at a Border's book signing in Bend, Oregon.

Below: Monty chatting to readers at a bookshop in Australia.

Monty with a youthful fellow horse lover at a demonstration.

Above: A young physically challenged student is encouraged by Monty during a visit he made to a therapeutic riding facility while on tour.

Below: Monty with a young friend.

Above: John Newton
from Exxon at a Flag is Up
corporate dinner.

Left: Monty and Pat
enjoying a dance together.

Above right: Monty waiting
to enter the arena during a
demonstration in Sydney.

Right: Monty lecturing a
group of students at his home
overlooking Flag is Up Farms.

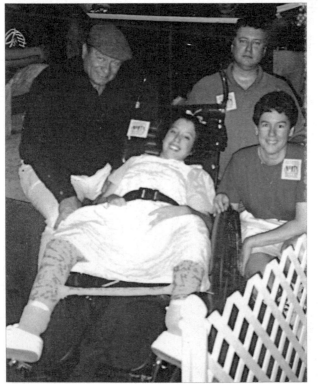

Above: Monty at a radio broadcasting studio taking call-in questions.

Left: A young fan meeting Monty at a demonstration of his methods.

Above right: A corporate group in the round pen, being introduced by Monty to the technique of Join-Up.

Right: Monty with a young admirer.

Clay Smith on Cadet, one of Monty's prized horses, and Jake Smith on Shy Boy, in the training yard at Flag is Up Farms.

high performance and was too inexperienced to really understand how to request it. Brownie taught me about contracts, which I have used both in my equine work and my work with children and adults.

Brownie was my primary horse in these contests, and though I entered him in virtually every category for Western-style riding, his speciality was an event called reining, which calls for the horse to work at speed. He must perform intricate maneuvers with only the slightest of signals from the rider. Brownie was an incredible stopper and he could turn really well. He was cooperative, energetic and generous, in virtually every aspect of his work, but his sliding stops were magic! Every horse, like every person, has his Achilles heel, and for Brownie it was his figure eights. To win in high-level competition, you must be sharp in all the phases of your discipline. Brownie and I were winning nearly every week, but I could see the competition getting tougher and our performances tailing off. Our figure eights were less than I wanted them to be and I just couldn't seem to keep his enthusiasm as high as I wanted. I consulted a couple of the old masters and both indicated to me they thought Brownie was tired. They felt he needed a rest in order to sharpen his responses.

I sat down and reflected on our training sessions and concluded that there was no question I was overtraining Brownie. He was jaded and going sour on his work. I was upset that I had allowed youthful enthusiasm to blind me to the needs and desires of my horse. I realized that I had wanted him to be just as good on Wednesday in a practice session as on Sunday in the finals. As his level of excellence waned, I had worked harder in an attempt to make him the perfect horse in every way and on every day.

I obviously hadn't yet learned how to temper the work sessions so as to keep my horse fresh and happy in mind, body and spirit. We humans often speed through life focused on our goals and kicking obstacles out of the way. The type A of our species is generally a high achiever and often becomes the boss. The boss will often fail to recognize the need for praise and recognition because he or she exists in a self-motivated bubble. People who rise to leadership positions are inherently self-motivated and tend to need little praise.

Employers, who may need little sleep and are intrinsically motivated, expect the same dedication from their employees, who are generally extrinsically motivated. We should spend more time establishing intrinsic motivation and make fewer outright demands. It is easy to make unreasonable demands of those we ask to perform for us. These demands stress employees, who have other needs to be met, which may, more likely than not, precede ours. Meeting our needs is an important part of our personal survival.

I can understand that Brownie was pressured, perhaps beyond the limits of what he felt he was able to give me. I trespassed into the energy reserve that was his alone and his intrinsic motivation flagged as a result. Employers often make the same mistake, and if that happens they should quickly discover their employees' need, look for solutions and negotiate.

A cowboy has a tendency to call upon his best horse when there is a job to be done. He is comfortable with him and confident that he will complete the task. The cowboy's natural inclination is, therefore, to use the chosen animal until it is simply too tired to perform. It seems to me we often do this in the workplace with our best employees. We need to be aware of this, to be quick to reward outstanding performance and to be diligent in requiring underachievers to perform at higher levels.

I was cleaning stalls one morning and Brownie's stall was the last one in the line. I probably didn't do a very good job on the stalls that particular morning because I was anxious to get to his. While cleaning his stall, I had a conversation with Brownie, which marked a turning point in my perception of the word "partnership."

"Brownie, if I could speak your language, what I'd say is that if we could somehow strike a deal, I would set you free to practice at your pace, Monday through Friday. I wouldn't press you as much as I have in the past, if you could guarantee me a superb performance on Saturday and Sunday. I have been putting too much pressure on you and I believe I have stolen your enthusiasm for the work we are doing. I intend to change and become more aware of your needs. I still expect the very best from you, but I think I have been unreasonable in the recent past."

Brownie, of course, couldn't understand a word I was saying; I was talking to myself, but I was the only one who needed to hear it anyway. I stopped pushing him so hard during the week. Brownie did regain his enthusiasm and we went on to win many more championships.

Today I am often asked for advice about problems with horses. People will start off by saying, "I've got a stupid horse." As soon as I hear this, I have a strong suspicion about where the problem lies. It is all too often with the person, not the horse. There is significant educational value in looking inward, asking ourselves what we have done to contribute to the problem, whether dealing with people or horses.

Remember, horses were doing just fine for approximately 47 million years before the emergence of *Homo sapiens*. My answer is there are no problem horses, only horses that have problems with the actions of people.

INTRINSIC VERSUS EXTRINSIC LEARNING

Extrinsic = coming from outside
Intrinsic = coming from within

In this section I intend to deal with the two major categories of learning, intrinsic and extrinsic. When I use the term "learning intrinsically" I mean being self-motivated to find and absorb knowledge. By extrinsic learning I mean a process that uses some outside motivation, such as an examination or fear of failure, to force learning to take place. Extrinsic learning encompasses any external force other than the desire from within to learn. The whip is a typical external force used to motivate a horse. In the case of the classroom, the ruler on the back of the hand would be in the same category.

There is no question that horses can be trained extrinsically, by breaking their will to resist. Traditional training methods have produced cavalry for war and the horses that cleared and then ploughed our lands, served as our transportation and even delivered our mail.

The days of 100 lashes for offenses against society are, in most civilized countries, a thing of the past. Corporal punishment is no longer utilized in most military training, schools or penitentiaries. But strangely enough the whip is still an important item sold in tack shops. It seems that although we no longer believe that lashing out violently against other human beings is an acceptable form of education, we still consider it effective where horses are concerned, even though studies have shown that the whip is not a useful discipline for either flight animals or humans.

Over the ages one of the activities of Equus has been to entertain man. Racing, for example, has been a favorite sport for thousands of years, and so far we have felt it necessary to use a whip in the execution of our races. The fact is that horses run slower when they are whipped than when they are not. Yet you will often see horses return from a race with large welts across their fleshy quarters. People who engage in racing will often tell you that they are involved in an activity that the horse enjoys. I believe that statement is true. They will go on to say that when the horse is only a few days old you will see it racing with other foals. This is nature's way of training and conditioning horses as part of the survival process. If the young horse didn't find joy in running from a very early age, he would be taken by predators before he reproduced, and he wouldn't bring into the world more horses with that same genetic makeup.

In my opinion, they do love to race, and I love racing. But we should take the whips out of racing, not only because they are inhumane, but because they are ineffective. A whipless race would produce a winner and a loser and there would be some in the middle. Guess what? That is what happens now. From a genetic standpoint a horse that would race and win for the love of it is more valuable to the owner and the breed itself than the horse that requires a whip.

When I discuss this issue around the world, I often describe the following scenario: in a discussion with the track coach at a local high school, you might suggest that his best miler just isn't running fast enough. He isn't giving his all. You advise the coach: "I believe I can show you how to get this young man to give you more effort in the final 200 meters or so and thus turn in a faster time. What I propose to you is that I will ride in the back of a pick-up truck and I will take a long buggy whip with me. We will drive alongside your athlete and when I believe that he is giving less than his best effort, I will use the whip across his backside. He will speed his pace and reduce his total time." The coach would justifiably ask you to leave the campus or have you arrested. He might point out that he has spent two or three years helping this young man develop his running form. The movement of his arms, his stride, even subtleties such as the position of his chin and the focus of his eyes come into play.

"How can you possibly suggest," this coach might say, "that causing pain to a young man while he is performing could do anything but take his mind off the task at hand? It is ludicrous to think that this could be effective." He might go on, "How could you possibly think that a stinging whip would improve his performance?"

I submit to you that it is no different for horses, and we must work to eliminate this barbaric treatment.

•

So far I have described an extrinsic form of training; now let us explore what I believe to be a far more effective form of learning, intrinsic.

Young human beings are instinctively resentful of force and domination, which includes verbal as well as physical punishment. Most of the time young victims of abuse will choose one of two paths. Some will knuckle under and become timid, reserved, even reclusive. It is sad to see people in this condition because circumstances have stolen a normal life from them. And the majority of victims of overt violence will act out aggressively and develop violent tendencies of their own.

It might seem logical that a child who had been beaten would disdain violence and therefore fail to engage in it himself. It just doesn't work out that way. It appears that when adults in the child's life use violence as a course of action, they imprint in the child's brain the idea that violence is an effective way to deal with problems. In later life, the victim generally tends to rise quickly to anger and use violence as an instant solution to his own problems—a repetitive pattern that causes violence to occur generation after generation. I am working hard to prove that a victim of domestic violence can become nonviolent and consciously rule it out of his or her life. I am testimony to the fact that the chain of violence can be broken.

I have said many times that there is no such thing as teaching, only learning, and fear-based methods of imparting information are not as effective as those that use intrinsic, self-motivated learning. If the student takes on information willingly, there is a good chance he will remember it.

Over the decades, racehorses have taught me that it is far more effective to train them by giving them a reason to want to run rather than telling them that they have to run. Imagine putting a horse in the starting stall, with a few others to compete against. Next you push the button that causes the gates to fly open, freeing the horses to run forward. The traditional trainer often hits the horse over the hips the moment the gates are released. The jockey might yell out and use his body to press the horse forward into immediate flight. All the horses race ahead while rolling their eyes back to see if they can determine where the sharp pain came from.

Most horses will eventually accept this extrinsic goad, but it is far less effective than the intrinsic alternative, which would be to quietly walk the horse into the stall, placing one or two older, more experienced horses with him. When the gates are opened, I want my people to remain calm and quiet. The older horses leave immediately while the inexperienced one might linger, not knowing what is expected of him. He will watch the other horses as they leave, and he will generally follow even if tentatively and slowly.

The riders on the older horses have previously been instructed to slow down their mounts after the break and let them just canter along at a slow pace. Once the young horse is fifty feet or so clear of the gate, then and only then will his rider begin to encourage him to go forward at a higher rate of speed. The young horse will see the older ones and perceive them as competition. He will begin to run faster and faster, with his rider pressing him past the slow-moving horses, causing him to think he is the leader of the herd.

The next time this young horse is taken to the starting gate, he will have a greater awareness of the situation. The horse that was treated extrinsically will probably be reluctant to go into the stall and will stand nervously, but the intrinsically motivated horse will be happy to go in and looks forward every time to competing. The second time around, the young horse still finds his rider quiet as can be. When the gates spring open he reacts more quickly and passes the older horses earlier than he did the first time. I find that three or four of these educational sessions will generally produce a racing prospect far more effective at the starting gate than the extrinsically motivated horse. He will also be more likely to accept the starting gate throughout his career without resentment, and cause fewer problems. He will generally start faster because he wants to perform, and not because he is forced to.

The starting-stall scenario should be viewed as a metaphor for the treatment of human beings, whether they are infants with families, people in the workplace or those locked up in prisons. I believe that virtually every human being wants to be accepted, respected and loved. If we are given a chance to impress our peers with positive actions and positive consequences result from those actions, we are likely to follow a productive track. Often I am called to all parts of the world to work with horses that have become negative at the starting gate because of extrinsic forces. It is far more difficult to deal with individuals—horses or people— who have taken the law into their own hands than with those who are young and unspoiled.

The horses are no different from the children I meet. If they are angry and violent from the outset, I introduce them to my contract system, described below. It is a challenge to set up an environment in which I may gain their trust and convince them that by removing violence you will cause them to want to perform. I look for any little positive thing that they do and congratulate them profusely for that.

THE BLACKBOARD SYSTEM

For decades now I have used a system (see pages 216–19) that has worked well to provide parents with an objective way of dealing with the behavior of their children. I've used the system both within my own family (my wife, Pat, and I have raised more than three dozen children and young people) and in working with others. Early on in its development I gave it a name, "The Blackboard System." By its very title, you can see that it preceded the wonderful white boards they have these days that require felt markers and stay nice and clean. No messy chalk or squeaks that set your teeth on edge.

The Blackboard System evolved directly from my conversation with Brownie. Brownie helped me understand that if you can give your student the chance to choose his or her own consequences you will instill a sense of responsibility over his or her own actions—taking yourself out of the punishment business. Once I'd embraced this notion, the more horses I trained, the more Brownie's lesson was reaffirmed. The rapidly increased learning curve of one young horse after another would inform me that it was working well. I had horses like Mischief, Dan Tack and many others that verified the contract system.

Once the horses taught me, through their own actions, how it worked, I knew I could apply the same methods to the young people we began to bring into our home. Naturally, there were aspects of this system that changed when applied to human students, but it amazed me how easily it translated from Equus to English.

The essential elements of this system are as follows: each child has two boards that are about two feet by three feet. These belong to both parent and child and are placed in a prominent position where it is easy for both to view them without difficulty. I prefer to have them outside the child's room, and in an area that is open to the entire family.

The primary objective of this system is to bypass the parent as the administrator of discipline or punishment. It sets up a contract whereby child and parent bilaterally agree on the response to positive or negative behavior. A secondary goal (possibly even more important) is to bring the young person to an understanding of contracts and responsibilities. I have found this system extremely effective in educating young people in the principle "My word is my bond." There was a time when a high percentage of people lived by this theory. It could have been the rural nature of the environment where I was raised, but I can recall a time when shaking a man's hand while looking him in the eye was considered more binding than today's legal contracts. It would be wonderful if that were still the case today. Unfortunately it is not. Can you imagine, however, how much better a chance your children would have in life if that became a guiding principle for them? Today, with integrity in such short supply, your child could be a real hero if people knew they could count on his word. And almost all children can be helped by the contract system.

It is not a bad idea if the two boards you supply to each child are a different color, or identified by different frames or some other distinguishing feature. A different visual appearance dramatizes the different content of the boards.

One board should be labeled POSITIVE and the other NEGATIVE. In addition, the names of the child and parents should appear on both boards. The clear implication is that one board will deal with the positive factors of the child's life and the other with the negative. Further, it clearly establishes that the young person and the parent are involved with the board and its objectives.

It is critical that the parent first sit down with the child and calmly talk through this procedure, allowing no emotion to come into the explanation. Initiating this system should never appear to the child to be the act of a desperate parent who is seeking some bizarre method of dealing with the problems of their relationship. I recommend that parents explain to the child that they feel they have not been altogether fair in the past and that it is now time to put their relationship on a more positive course. The parents should indicate that they feel that the principles of this system will be an improvement for both the child and the parents. Furthermore, the parents should make it abundantly clear that there will never be a rule to deal with negative consequences unless there is a counterpoint—a positive consequence to a positive action.

Before putting this system into effect, it is always helpful if the child views the procedure as a chance to get more out of life than he or she did before. When properly carried out, I have found this procedure to be easily the most useful tool for achieving successful parent-child relationships I have seen in over forty years of observing them.

Obviously it is the parent's obligation to mold the program to fit the needs of the child in question appropriately. A two-year-old girl clearly sits at the opposite end of the spectrum from a seventeen-year-old boy. A shy, reserved individual who has difficulty meeting people has very different needs from those of the outgoing youngster who never perceives anyone as a stranger. It is also critical to consider your geographical location. There will be significant differences in lifestyle between a family living in a town or the suburbs and one living in the country.

Once the principles of this practice have been fully understood by both parties, it is time to sit down, go to work on the boards and put them into effect. I recommend that you deal with the positive board first. The parent should consider carefully all the aspects I have alluded to above and then decide on a shortlist of positive consequences. I recommend the blackboard system for children as young as two years old, despite the fact that they may not be able to read or write. The parent can describe what's on the board and then, taking the child's hand with the marker, help the child place his or her initials under a one-line contract. It is amazing what young brains can comprehend.

The parent then initials the contract as well. After signing, the parent should make eye-to-eye contact with the child, shake hands and say, "We now have a contract." Imagine, for example, that we are dealing with Sally, a four-year-old. Sally takes a delight in spitting at people. The positive contract might say:

> *No spitting at anyone for two full days and I*
> *will take you to visit your grandma.*

You read it to Sally, and each of you initials the contract and you shake hands. Next you deal with the negative board, which might say:

> *If you spit on anyone within the next two days,*
> *you will scrub one tile in the shower.*

You read it again, each sign it and shake hands. I find it much better to list an action that must be completed rather than selecting a forfeit that would prevent the child from doing something she enjoys, although parents may decide that as a negative consequence a child should be restricted from watching cartoons or playing with friends. If they feel that this is the most effective discipline, then there is nothing terribly wrong with it, as long as no discipline is carried out for an unreasonable length of time, which in itself would then become abusive. It should be noted at this point that I do not recommend food or money on either side of the blackboard.

We all know that Sally is not going to be very effective at cleaning any of the tiles in the shower, but that is not our purpose. (Obviously, young people need constant supervision and should use only mild soap and water, never toxic or abrasive cleaners.) Make it clear to the child that he or she is working as a negative consequence. I have found this to be an effective negative activity for tiny children because they can complete the procedure fairly easily and without creating an enormous mess. Sally should be notified that should the negative behavior persist, the number of tiles will be increased.

The parent has *no excuse* for not going to Grandma's house if Sally doesn't spit. And there is no reason why she should not clean the tile if she does. Some children will attempt to control the parent by throwing a tantrum when faced with the prospect of cleaning a tile or some other chore. I suggest that, just as I do with my horses when they act out in a negative fashion, the parent simply step back and smile. (Because while smiling you are less likely to think of harsh measures to deal with obstreperous behavior.) The parents needs to hold fast to the belief that they are doing the right thing—a tantrum is part of the training procedure and should be viewed as such. When the tantrum is over, then the child cleans the tile.

Parents must judge how far to press the issue of cleaning the tile. Begin by accepting the slightest positive you can find and then reward the child by stating she has completed the task. I recommend that the parent or guardian view this moment as a victory, give the child a hug and say "I love you," letting her know that you are members of the same team.

It is incredible how effective parents can be when creating paths for children to follow. Lifelong patterns of behavior can be established. My brother was a picky eater. I, on the other hand, got praise from my parents for eating everything in sight. My mother often said, "Monty is a very good little boy. He always eats up his food." I learned very quickly that the more I ate the more praise I received, and my brother was often asked why he couldn't be good like Monty and finish his meal. This initiated a lifelong pattern: even in my sixties I have a hard time leaving any-thing on my plate, despite my doctor's insistence that I cut down my food intake! The psychology of positive reinforcement is most effective and parents need to thoughtfully reinforce the paths they would like their children to follow.

Let us return now to the conclusion of the second day. Did Sally spit on someone or did she refrain from doing so? We will first assume that Sally was a good little girl and that, while you closely observed her, she did not act in this negative fashion. You may well have seen a movement or two when Sally appeared to be thinking about it, but then she decided to refrain. That is good. The parent should not get involved in either encouraging a posi-tive decision or discouraging a negative one. It is important that the parent remember that it is the child's decision that is important.

It is important to designate a specific time when this particular contract is completed. If Sally arrived at the designated time with-out committing the negative act, I recommend that the parent take the time to shake her hand, look her in the eye and congratu-late her on her victory with another hug and a big smile, which never hurts. The child should feel loved and accepted by the par-ent and feel that the presence of the parent has created a place of safety for her. And don't forget to agree together on a time for the enactment of the positive consequence—the visit to Grandma's house.

When you are at Grandma's house, I strongly suggest you say, in the presence of the child and her Grandma, "Sally has been a good little girl." Make it clear in her presence that she is being rewarded for good behavior. The parent need not mention the negative behavior because it would only be a source of embarrass-ment. Any discipline that demeans or shames the child falls into the same category as corporal punishment. It is extrinsic rather than intrinsic training.

Let us now consider the negative outcome. Since the contract was clear and concise it is evident what should happen the moment the child spits on someone. If at all possible, the negative consequences should begin immediately. If the child chooses a time when you are away from your home, it will be necessary to wait, but the negative aspects of the contract should come into effect as soon as possible. The moment the child spits the parent should appear sorrowful, *never angry*. It is important to let the child know that you are disappointed about this outcome. Since, however, it was the child's decision, you, the parent, are essentially outside or detached from that decision process and are also affected by the contract in a negative way.

It is essential for a child to feel loved and accepted, but to be made aware that you are very sorry that she has not lived up to the contract and must carry out the negative consequence. Remind her that you are very sorry that she has to do this and stay with her as she scrubs the tile. You should leave the child with your hope that she will be more successful with her contracts in the future.

It is critical that the parent not be discouraged by early contractual failures. They are, in fact, as important to the learning process as contractual success. If a parent is experiencing an extremely high percentage of successes, it is quite possible that he is not setting the goals high enough for the child. I believe that he should then increase his expectation by raising the standards, remembering that when you increase the negative consequences, you must also create the potential for greater reward.

The principles of this system are the same when dealing with all ages, sexes and lifestyles. The number of issues dealt with is also important. I have learned over the years that the parent or adult should begin with one, two or three issues and then expand this number only when it is clear that the child is handling the process well. Obviously the older child who is thought to be relatively normal will be able to cope with more issues than a very young child or one who is troubled to a significant degree.

One of the most frequently asked questions regarding my contract system is "What do I do when my child simply says, 'I'm not going to do it!'?" The answer is first to smile, then gently reestablish that so long as there are negative consequences left undone there can be no positive consequences. The negative board must be entirely cleared off before any rewards can be reaped from the positive board. It should be understood from the outset that a refusal to live up to the contract places the child in a position whereby he has no privileges whatsoever. Until the contract is fulfilled the child's life is restricted.

I often recommend to parents that in addition to the contract boards, they can bilaterally agree with the youngster that certain actions are completely unacceptable. For example, the teenager and parent may agree that shooting or stabbing another person is not an option. Hitting another person with a heavy object is also totally unacceptable. Parent and child may go on to agree that stealing or taking hard drugs will simply not be a part of their existence. You may even agree that so-called lighter drugs must never be used. Parents can attach to these bilateral agreements any consequences they deem appropriate. I often suggest that the parents should agree with the child that drugs and violence won't be a part of their own life either: this is simply a part of being good role models. Young people admire a parent's willingness to enter into an agreement like this, fully prepared to accept the negative consequences.

I remember one negative example that took place in a family with a boy and a girl. The boy found nothing wrong with borrowing his sister's bicycle and as boys will do he would ride with other boys and bring the bike home very muddy. The girl, about twelve years of age, was using the bicycle to ride to school. It was a girl's bike that worked well riding with a dress, it was just that when she got to school she had a muddy dress and soiled books and binder. The father, watching what was going on, began to give his son the obligation of washing his sister's bicycle as a negative consequence. Several lessons were learned with this innovative contract. First, the son had an effective negative consequence for whatever action was agreed to on his board. Second, the son was able to learn a very good lesson about taking care of other people's property that you borrow. Third, the daughter was able to attend school with a clean dress and books. Finally, whenever the boy borrowed his sister's bicycle he kept it out of the mud as much as possible.

When working with teenagers the consequences, both negative and positive, take on quite different dimensions from those outlined in the initial example. Again I suggest that parents try to stay with things to do rather than things not to do and to eliminate food or money, when possible, from the list of consequences.

In our part of the world I have found one of the most positive consequences for the teenage boy is taking him fishing. It is generally a quiet time together, takes place in pleasant surroundings and allows parent and child to have ample time for calm and reflective conversation, which in itself often produces positive results. Hiking, camping, going to a ball game or even a movie or a play will often serve a teenage boy well. I have not included horseback riding because, even though I obviously think it is a wonderful reward, it may not be appropriate for a very high percentage of readers of this book. If a parent does ride, it is certainly advisable to instruct the child in riding and use this activity wherever you can.

Although the teenage girl may enjoy many of the same activities as the teenage boy, the activity should always be tailored to the child. What the parent likes to do should not be terribly important in the selection process. This is a generalization, but teenage girls love movies, clothes and parties, too. Also, remember how much teenage girls love horses. These wonderful animals can be a very vital positive influence in the life of a teenage girl, if circumstances allow.

On the negative side of the blackboard, teenagers can mow lawns, paint fences and dig ditches. Bathroom scrubbing and painting are great allies to the city parent looking for negative consequences. It should be noted that normal chores that are a regular part of the family routine should not count when it comes to producing items to go on the negative consequences list.

A STORY

The Trouble with Harry

In March of 1975, I had about sixty head of two-year-olds in training at the Hollywood Park Race Track in Inglewood, California. Inglewood is the city where Los Angeles International Airport is located and is in one of the roughest urban areas of the Los Angeles basin. The racetrack is an oasis in the middle of a densely populated inner-city environment. Work at Hollywood Park starts each day well before sun-up. Because training is restricted to a four-hour period between 6 A.M. and 10 A.M., one must maintain a rigorous schedule or you simply can't complete your work. My horses were going out in sets of eight and I rode a horse along with them so that I could sit close to the action to assess the performance of my equine students.

Hollywood Park provides an overseer (outrider) who is in charge of all of the activities that take place during these morning workouts. He enforces the rules and sees to it that horses and people conduct themselves in the safest way possible. He rides a highly trained horse so that he can catch and bring under control any

Thoroughbred that might unseat his rider and run uncontrollably on the racecourse. I have always had the greatest respect for these men. They work hard and risk injury every day to assist trainers, riders and horses.

In 1975, the outrider in question was called Jim. I arrived on a particular morning and sat beside him while my first set of horses went about their work. We exchanged greetings.

"I've been waiting for you," he said, "I hear that you work a lot with kids, and I've got one that's driving me crazy. His name is Harry and he is four years old. He is just plain mean. Not even five yet and he has already tried to kill two of the neighbor's children. I keep a gun in the house and he got hold of it, chasing one of the neighbor's kids while trying to make the thing work, but he just couldn't figure it out. Yesterday he found a broken beer bottle and cut another playmate because he was angry over a game of marbles. Harry hits his mother constantly and even uses foul language toward me. My wife and I have both spanked him many times, but it just doesn't seem to do any good. I think I am raising a serial killer or something. Is there any way you can be of help to me?"

I have to tell you that I sat there for a minute feeling as though the blood within me had turned cold. The very thought of a four-year-old expressing this kind of anger and aggression was sobering, to say the least.

I spent the balance of that morning explaining to Jim the blackboard system. After ten o'clock we drove six or eight miles to where he lived. It was a mobile home park where the vehicles were in very close proximity to each other, with the narrowest of streets running between them. I doubt if anybody knew how many children were in residence in this mini-community, but I can tell you that they were plentiful. I met Harry, and although he seemed relatively normal during a one-hour visit, I noticed that he was very rough on the family dog. In a small yard at the rear of the house, I also saw him attempt to hit a cat with a stone he had found in the garden. I met Harry's mother and I must say that I sensed a strong feeling of desperation within her. She told me in private while Jim was on the telephone that she felt her husband's hours had a good deal to do with the child's anger. Jim left the house at 3:30 A.M. each day. He normally returned around 11:00 A.M., got something to eat and took a nap for a few hours. At four o'clock he would return to the track to feed and care for his horses. Quite often she would then not see Jim until eleven or midnight. He would get involved with buddies during the evening chore time and about four nights a week he would end up at a local watering hole. He spent very little time with Harry, and Harry asked a lot of questions about where his father was.

The following morning I approached Jim and made a fairly strong attempt to get him to understand the value of spending time with Harry. I explained it was my belief that this would be the primary solution to the problems of this little boy. In actual fact, I was just as interested in helping Jim improve his life as in helping Harry.

Jim set up, under my supervision, one of the best blackboard procedures I have ever seen. He was very innovative in the selection of his consequences and the results were virtually immediate. It was the fourth day of the program when I rode out on the track and met Jim, who had a big smile on his face. "You won't believe this kid of mine," he said. "He is going so positive, I can't believe it."

Jim told me that Harry had come to him the night before and said, "Give me some more 'contacts,' Daddy, I want some more 'contacts.' "

"He doesn't even get the word right," Jim said, "but I can't believe how well the contracts are working with him."

Jim explained that Hollywood Park had stocked the two lakes in the infield with bass about eight years before. He said there were some real trophies out there and that the fish population had become much higher than the park wanted. Track officials were pleased to allow him and his son to fish there. "I set up some pretty tough consequences, but gave him a chance to go fishing. He caught two fish last night and has fallen in love with the sport."

About six weeks later, the day before I was to leave Hollywood Park and return to Flag Is Up, Jim came to me and thanked me, saying that Harry was a totally different child. He was still intense and filled with energy, but he had now turned it in a positive direction. Harry was fishing very well now with his own rod, which he used skilfully. He was learning to ride a horse and they had gone on hikes together in the mountains to the north of Los Angeles. Jim went on to tell me that his son was so positive now that in order to complete the contracts he has had to spend virtually every evening with Harry. His wife had begun making picnic suppers and bringing them to the track along with Harry. When he had finished caring for his horses, they would go to the infield for their little fishing trip. While Harry fished quite seriously, Jim spent time with his wife helping to set out their dinners. He came to the realization that he was under the influence of an alcohol habit that had gradually taken him away from his family.

"I am going to meetings, now," he said, "and getting some counseling. I can't figure out whether I saved Harry or Harry saved me and my marriage."

A STORY

Where Do I Sign?

I have found the contract system to be effective with virtually every age group of children. People have asked me whether signing a contract really works with young children. It does, as Harry's story showed and as Spencer's story will show. When dealing with infants there can be no written contract. We must forge our agreement through a consistent pattern of positive consequences for positive actions and always negative consequences for negative actions.

In 1999 a young mother approached me about her four-year-old son, Spencer. She was desperate to learn how to deal with his aggressive behavior toward his twin sister, Alice, and their baby-sitter. The mother explained to me that, based on what she had read in *The Man Who Listens to Horses*, she had tried a contract approach to deal with Spencer's hitting, kicking, spitting, nasty talk and other bad behavior. She had no success. Concerned about her dilemma, I spent some time talking to her about her approach. I learned that she had tried to cover every kind of negative behavior in one contract with a four-year-old! There were simply too many for the child to absorb and address.

A smart woman, the mother laughed when she realized her mistake. She went back, sat down with her two children and negotiated a contract dealing exclusively with one behavior problem— that of physical aggression. The contract stated that whenever any member of the family used physical aggression against anyone, the offender would choose to go to his or her room. Her husband and Spencer's twin sister immediately signed the contract. Spencer, however, refused. Even though he could not read, he clearly understood the nature of the agreement.

The mother later told me that at first she was dumbfounded, but she remembered what I had said about removing all positive consequences for negative actions. She told Spencer, "Well, if you don't want to sign and be part of the family's agreement about how we live together, we won't be able to do any fun things together either, such as going to your swimming lessons today."

"I don't want to go swimming," was his swift response.

The mother tried again, "Well, I guess we won't be able to go over to our friends' house either; no visiting Joe and Dorothy and no making cookies at their house."

Spencer considered that prospect for a moment, picked up the pen and signed. Then, he turned to his mother and said, "Let's go to Joe and Dorothy's house!"

She explained that they would all go to their friends' house the next weekend. In addition, she told Spencer and Alice that she would give them a tool, an important word—*conversation*. If they said the word *conversation*, she would agree to stop whatever she was doing and talk to them for as long as they needed about whatever had made them angry.

The mother also told me that she and her husband decided to spend at least one afternoon a week with each of the twins, one-on-one, so that the kids wouldn't feel the need to use aggressive behavior to get attention. She said that she had noted a marked improvement in Spencer's behavior and general demeanor. He no longer seemed as angry and ready to strike out. When I spoke to her last, she said the agreement was working fine, as long as she and her husband were consistent. For example, since the contract calls for the offender to choose to go to his or her own room, she couldn't forcibly put the child in his room. Instead, she had to continue removing privileges until it became easier for the child to enforce the rules of the contract than to disobey.

Sometimes it was inconvenient, as when she had to cancel a family hiking trip to stay home with Spencer, but she realized that if she stuck with it, her children would believe that her word was her bond and would be less inclined to continue testing her.

The family's experience demonstrates the value of a child learning that there are never positive consequences for negative actions. It was actually important, however, that Spencer also learned that he could get positive consequences when his actions were positive. Persistence is of paramount importance in applying these principles, and Spencer's program is a wonderful example of just how effective they are.

Six

THE GOOD PARENT

Let the child succeed,
let the child fail.

INFANTS

Throughout my formative years I was vitally interested in why creatures, human and animal, are the way they are. We can be separated by species or geographic location, by great psychological differences, but there is a clear interspecies relationship. We are linked through mutual dependence.

I hope this book shows that there is a closer tie between different species than most people have ever thought. My work indicates that there is a human-to-animal compatibility never before thought to exist, which in turn yields a whole new perspective on human relationships.

•

My formative years were 1935 through 1953. I would like to take a hard look with you at those early years from the standpoint of human psychology.

As for many people, the outbreak of World War II changed my life dramatically. The horse industry came to a standstill because of its nonessential nature. We were forced to move our horse facility to make space for Japanese-American prisoners. Many of my relatives and acquaintances went off to fight in the war and my father was forced to leave the horse business, taking a job as a policeman.

Although I was troubled by these changes, I had a strong underlying curiosity about psychology. I had a great need to know why the Japanese government, and Hitler and Mussolini, acted as they did. I was only six at the time of Pearl Harbor, and yet I was fascinated by news broadcasts on the radio. Edward R. Murrow, John Cameron Swazey and others were voices from the void, bringing news that both disturbed and intrigued me.

I am not interested in the subject of war. I have never been one to watch war movies, nor was I obsessed with firearms. My interest was in the mindset of people who made decisions with such wide-ranging and negative sociological implications.

As a young man I found violence perplexing. I had been influenced deeply by my father's traditional but harsh treatment of both his horses and me. The people around me worked to convince me that I should look to violence to deal with issues of life and that I should accept violence as part of my own educational process. When it was used in an attempt to control or mold my own behavior, I viewed it with resentment. Because of my deep sense of kinship with horses I constantly wondered if the horses felt the same. In my young mind I wanted to be good and do things right and found no encouragement from beatings or verbal violence. I found myself retreating to my horses, and interacting with them in an attempt to bring to my life some social order.

There is no question that horses had the most positive effect on my psychological development. Throughout grammar school I had no doubt that the behavior of Equus was closely connected to the behavior of man. I recall having discussions with teachers regarding the patterns of behavior in cattle, dogs, cats and even wild animals, which when carefully observed related distinctly to the psychology of the human race. There was little acceptance for my seemingly outlandish theories, which were sometimes ridiculed, but one teacher, Sister Agnes Patricia, supported and encouraged me to continue seeking with an open mind the answers for which I was intently searching.

At Hartnell college, and later at California State Polytechnic University, I volunteered for every field experiment that I could, particularly those involving the behavioral patterns of families. This was a fertile field for study as men returned from Korea to pick up their lives and get an education. They had seen or done some of the most violent things possible, and it was difficult for them to regain normality and return to a life with spouses and children.

In 1957 while attending the university, I was involved in a study on infants. I was amazed to discover the incredible early awareness of human beings, even in the first few months of life. I later came to realize that the adult horse and human infant have a great deal in common.

The human infant is capable of much more awareness and a higher level of comprehension than I ever dreamed. A child of eighteen months will challenge you to a far greater degree than a highly trained horse at its optimum age. When counselors involved in the study explained to young parents the fact that behavioral patterns are being formed in the first sixty days of life, back then, they found it very difficult to believe, though some forty years later we are very familiar with these ideas. They would argue with the counselor, pointing out that they felt that there was little awareness in a child of that age.

An enlightened child psychologist educated in the art of deciphering infant behavior can point out the most comprehensive reactions, responses and thought patterns in very young children so clearly they begin to seem nearly conversational.

During this time I came to believe that many of the young parents in our study groups had negatively affected the lives of their infants even before they were three months of age. The actions of adults, particularly parents, around an infant are critical in these early days of life. Loud noises, particularly shouting, for instance, whether related to the child or not, can negatively impact development. It leads the child to feel that he is not in a safe place and increases adrenaline levels in the child, which causes worry. Shouting is not only stressful psychologically, but it stresses the infant physiologically as well.

Failing to spend sufficient bonding time can be detrimental to healthy development. In addition to a tranquil environment, an infant requires a feeling of family. In order to enjoy normal development the child must have a sense of security that there are adults around him to see to his every need. The human species is born into a state of (relative) helplessness and needs to feel cared for and protected.

Horses are similarly vulnerable. Experiments show that very young horses exposed to loud disturbing sounds and deprived of mother bonding develop peptic ulcers at four or five times the normal rate. In addition, such young horses tend to be far more nervous and unreliable than those given acceptable environments during the early months.

If the principal adults in the young human's life fail to create a space of safety, negative patterns of behavior will almost assuredly be created within that tiny brain. On the other hand parents who take advantage of this window of opportunity make these early days a time of great joy. Enlightened parents will come to understand that their influence is creating a child who is likely to become a well-adjusted and happy adult.

The process is similar to that of foal imprinting, which I described earlier, and which, if properly done, can help the horse throughout his life accept the human being as nonpredatorial. It is my opinion that in the next twenty years or so we will find foal imprinting to be a most important addition to the horse world.

Working with horses is best done when you make positive behavior easy and negative behavior difficult; this applies to the human as well. Horses, like humans, should be responsible for their own actions, including the consequences of those actions. I train my horses by allowing them to follow the path of least resistance. This creates a window through which they can pass, one leading in a direction that is positive. This same theory applies to the newborn child.

Parents who subscribe to my concepts should learn to be consistent to the letter with their children. Parents who give mixed messages are on the path to failure. Infants can be beset by mixed messages quite possibly to an even greater degree than children, adolescents or adults. If a parent has outlined a negative consequence for the breaking of a particular rule, then it is absolutely imperative that there is follow through. If a promise is made as a reward, there is absolutely no excuse for not keeping it.

Many parents fail to stand fast, not seeing that this can have negative consequences on a child. Incredibly enough, this is extremely important for infants, even in the first few months of life. These tiny human beings will observe and respond to circumstances. Although they do not have the cognitive ability to plan a course of action, adults often do it for them by unintentionally encouraging negative behavior.

If the infant cries the parent should immediately make sure there is no physical discomfort: hunger, soiled diaper, too hot or too cold, etc. Should the adult discover an element of discomfort, then the child has learned a valuable lesson: "I can signal adults when I am in need. I can summon their assistance by the means I have just used." But what if the adult found no physical reason for the child to act negatively? I have talked to many parents who hurry to pick up a child screaming in a fit of anger. They will pick him up, walk with him, talk softly and humor him until he is relaxed and put him back down once more. They rationalize that they love their child and can't stand to see it unhappy. They feel cruel allowing the child to cry without picking it up. The fact is they are training the infant to demand immediate attention any time it chooses and for whatever reason. And they may be building up trouble for the teenage years. If five minutes or so of negative action is watched over (and watching over the child is essential in case the child's cries do indicate a serious problem or sickness; and if prolonged crying sessions are frequent, consult a family doctor) but not responded to, generally the child will go to sleep or settle into a tranquil state.

As a parent, one waits with great anticipation for that moment when the child goes through a tantrumlike episode and then calms down. When that does happen, immediately pick up the infant and hold him close, if possible bare skin to bare skin. This moment of bonding can be vital to the healthy development of this tiny individual. Speak softly, massage, possibly using warm oil, count fingers and toes and come forth with expressions of love and warmth. This is a precious moment and is almost as effective for the parent as it is for the child. Properly done I've found that parents often grow more attached to the child and are far less likely to act out in anger later on.

I have talked with many parents who have worked hard at understanding these principles and then can't seem to control situations that occur when, for instance, they take the child to the home of the grandparents. Grandparents often will say that they are there to spoil the child and they don't really see the need for this type of behavior shaping. I believe it is critical that all of the adults influencing the infant understand the principles by which it is being raised. Mixed signals are detrimental to the future of any young person.

In the preceding scenario the infant comes to understand two valuable lessons. The first is that he can summon the assistance of adults at a time of physical discomfort. The second is that he will receive clearly defined reward for positive behavior. These elements of understanding are formed at this early age. I believe that caring parents, both mothers and fathers, should set time aside and encourage this kind of interaction. Working parents in particular often have demanding schedules and I recommend budgeting time to do this. It is still often left to the mother to encourage the father by way of arranging the time and talking it through. Many fathers still find this difficult, but all fathers I know who have experienced it become strong advocates later on, and I have often been told that these sessions with their infants were probably the most important moments and time in their lives.

SPARE THE ROD

I have interviewed literally hundreds of parents, and it is interesting to note how perceptions of parenthood, discipline, punishment and the proper rearing of a child vary greatly throughout our society. Too often when I ask an adult, "Are you a good parent?" I will get the response: "You bet I am. I make them toe the line."

This is a response that tells me a lot about their attitude toward parenting. You can see the similarity with traditional horsemanship, which embraces the theme, "You do what I tell you to or I'll hurt you," or "Hurt them before they hurt you," or "If you don't make them toe the line, you will just spoil them." Let us take a moment to investigate that parent and his mindset.

The person who is certain that he or she is a good parent is, in my opinion, very likely not. "You bet I am" has a ring of certainty to it, and a good parent realizes that the only measure of success is what sort of adult the rearing process produces. The good parent will most often respond by saying, "I try to be. I think I am," or "I don't know." Parents certain that they are making all the right decisions will often live to discover that they were either too demanding or too lenient.

The second part of the response, "I make them toe the line," is even more graphically demonstrative. These parents significantly lack the skills with which to optimize the chances of success. Such parents need to realize that it is virtually impossible to force the young human being to do anything, particularly over the long term. Most parents can make the youngster do what they want a few times through fear, just as the traditional trainer can frighten an otherwise physically superior creature into compliance. The whip is effective in the short term, but in the long term the infliction of pain only serves to create an enemy, to build resentment and destroy trust. The infliction of pain is the embodiment of "fast is slow" and is the antithesis of all that my methodology is based upon.

Remedial horses such as Blushing ET are examples of antisocial underachievers. If that horse had been a person, he would eventually have climbed a tower to shoot at defenseless pedestrians. The dominating and violent parent who doles out punishment liberally will very often raise a child who is either aggressive or submissive and underachieving.

An example of one of those mixed messages was brought home to me recently while I was on a radio show. The host had read my first book, and although the radio station had invited me to be his guest, I'm not sure he was particularly happy with that decision. "I enjoyed your book," he said, "but I must tell you that I strongly disagree with you in one area." "And what is that?" I asked.

"I am a religious man and I believe in the Bible and the Bible implies, 'If you spare the rod, you will spoil the child.' I don't believe you can raise a kid right unless you give them a good whipping every now and then. They have got to know who is boss and they have got to respect you."

I sat there for a moment, totally taken off guard. He was misquoting the Bible (and actually quoting a seventeenth-century poet who *enjoins* us to "spare the rod and spoil the child"), but he had the Old Testament point from Proverbs clear enough. I enquired as to his children's ages. He replied, "Ten, eight and five." I thought how foolish his statement was regarding his demand for *respect* and remarked to myself that he might see it as respect, but to his children it spelled F-E-A-R.

My position is that not everything in the Bible is to be taken literally, and I offer people a strictly tongue-in-cheek interpretation that the Biblical reference is to a fishing rod and not a whipping rod: that if you wait for a child to do something right and take him fishing, he'll learn a great deal more than if you wait for him to do something wrong and whip him for it.

You can chide me for my interpretation of the "Good Book," but I am a strong believer in positive reinforcement. I sincerely believe that the parent, guardian or foster parent who uses the positive side of the contract system to give reward and congratulations for something done well will maximize his or her chances of raising a well-adjusted adult.

A STORY

The Water Glass

At one time a boy of nine, who was interested in having a career with horses, lived with Pat and me as a foster child. He was intent on having his own horse to ride and to be the only person responsible for his care. He said it would be his own project, and that he would look after the animal in every way. I told him he would have to keep him in a designated spot and this area should be kept clean. If he were to ride the horse, he should also feed, water and groom it. He was so excited at the prospect, he willingly agreed to my contract. As long as a contract is decided on and adhered to, it can work well even without the blackboards. Consistency is the key.

Within a couple of weeks I noticed that the horse was without water. It was midday and very hot. The horse was uncomfortable and was pawing near the water bucket. On this particular occasion I made a decision to water the horse myself. I didn't want him to stand through the day without water until the boy came home from school at about three o'clock. Upon his arrival, I took him to the horse, sat him down and explained what had happened. He was quiet, but I could see he was very upset. He promised that it would not happen again. At that point I showed him a small water glass from the kitchen, which I had brought to the stable. I explained to him that we should expand on our contract. The next time he forgot to water the horse, I would not come to his rescue. When he got home from school, he would be obliged to water the horse using the glass to carry the water from the faucet to the bucket. He would have to keep bringing water from the faucet to the bucket until the horse was satisfied and the bucket was full. Keep in mind that this only had to be done if he neglected to water the horse. It was an agreement that had *negative consequences* only when there were *negative actions*. I said I hoped that he would never have to use the glass. I placed it on a shelf in the tackroom, confident that the boy would never have to touch it.

He agreed readily, because he had no intention of forgetting another time, but within three weeks it happened again. This time I left the horse as he was and at three o'clock when the boy arrived home, he realized his mistake. I was able to commiserate with him.

I had no call to become angry because the outcome of his mistake had been prearranged. Under the blackboard system I was not imposing punishment; this was self-administered, or intrinsic, discipline. He was very angry with himself, not at me. He simply went to the tackroom, got the glass and started to water the horse in the prescribed manner.

That evening he was still out there, painstakingly filling up the bucket. The horse was so thirsty that he promptly slurped up every glassful dropped into the container. For a few hours the boy couldn't make any headway.

When it was time for bed, Pat went out again to see how he was getting on. She came back and told me she didn't think he was going to make it. "He looks exhausted and is still trying to fill up the bucket with that glass."

It is really important to remember that when rearing young people you must always be honest with yourself and the child. You must never give way on discipline that you have agreed upon or you will undo the good that it would have accomplished.

I went to the barn to make sure that he wasn't in any danger. He was certainly tired and still angry with himself, but not in physical straits. I asked him if he thought I should allow him to stop before the job was completed. He said no, that he would complete his contract. I told him that was fine, because our word should always be our bond. By then the bucket was almost three-quarters full and the horse ceased drinking.

I stayed with him until the bucket was nearly full. At that point I put my arm around his shoulder, and we walked back to the house together. I told him how proud I was that he had accepted responsibility for his actions. I also explained that it was my sincere hope that the glass could now sit there, forever untouched. I told him that I loved him enough to help him to learn from this mistake.

Today, this young man is one of the most responsible individuals I know. He is now in his thirties, a college graduate and successful in his own business. His story shows how a negative can be turned into a positive, how discipline can be administered without anger and how a young person can administer that discipline himself without blaming the adult involved in any way. It is also easy to prearrange a reward for responsible behavior—soon afterward the young man earned, through another contract, the privilege of going on a fishing trip.

I make such a contract with every horse that enters a round pen with me. I never have to resort to anger or impulsive behavior. Both the negative and positive aspects of the contract work for the good of the relationship.

A STORY

There Are No Back Doors in Life

At the conclusion of my college years Pat and I began to take on the responsibility of foster children. For many reasons, it was informally agreed with parents that we would raise their children alongside our own. My interest in family relationships continued while I trained horses, competed on a regular basis and studied the psychology of Equus.

Meanwhile, a married couple who lived nearby in Paso Robles had also begun to take in foster children to live with them in a ranch setting. The following story is an interesting illustration of the outcome of giving positive consequences for negative actions.

The couple took on a seventeen-year-old by the name of David who wanted to live in the country and learn more about animals, agriculture and living with nature. He came from an upper-middle-class family, which seemed to be normal in every way—the couple was friendly with his parents. He was one of three children; his sister had already graduated from college and he had a younger brother. All three were above average students and had no apparent behavioral problems.

The arrangement went well for about nine months until David met some students from his school who were in the fast-living set. He was encouraged by them to party more than the foster parents felt was appropriate for his age. He often stayed out too late and consequently couldn't get up in the morning, and his schoolwork began to suffer. They were quick to start a program whereby he had to pay appropriate consequences for his negative actions. They had him doing extra work when he failed his curfew, was absent from school or late for chores in the morning.

He wasn't entirely happy with this, but they seemed to be making good progress. In early April he informed them that a formal dance was set for the third week in May. They were quick to give him permission to go to the event and took him to town to rent a tuxedo for the occasion. However, they told him that he was going to have to be responsible and get his schoolwork done, as well as his chores, and be home at night at a reasonable hour or he would not be allowed to go to the dance.

During the ensuing month he had one significant setback about the third week in April. He was asked to be home on a particular evening by eleven o'clock and it wasn't until four in the morning that he arrived with a serious amount of alcohol onboard. They let him sleep for about two hours and then got him up to do his chores. They went with him and explained to him that he was going to have to fulfill his obligations already agreed to and that, as a further consequence, if he should do this kind of thing once more before the prom date, he would not be going. The tuxedo could just hang where it was and he could stay home and do chores instead. The foster parents admonished him to advise his intended date that she would not have a dance partner if he broke the rules once more. He paid the price for his mistake, and they were back on track and doing quite well once again.

One week before the event he decided to stay out all night once more. When he came home, it was almost daylight; they again expressed disappointment and told him that they were very unhappy for him because, as their agreement stated, he would not be going to the dance. They told him that they had nothing to do with the decision that he had made to deny himself the privilege of going, and that he should notify his date as soon as possible.

David telephoned his parents to see if he could get the decision reversed. Shortly thereafter his mother called the foster parents to say that David should be allowed to go to the dance. They explained to her how important it was to stand behind agreements made. He had had a chance to go to this event and knew that they wanted him to go, but he had consciously broken their trust and traded away his right to attend the party. His mother felt that they should think up some other discipline and allow him to go. They were very upset by this and did their best to persuade her to change her mind, but were not successful.

The next day they got a call from the father, who also wanted them to change their minds and let David attend the dance. With both parents on the phone, the foster parents expressed their belief that this was a decision that would affect him negatively well into the future. It would lead him to conclude that there are back doors in life and that you don't have to be responsible for your actions. They felt it was a very big mistake.

David did go to the dance, and there were no other disciplinary measures, because the foster parents sent him home. The decision of the parents had placed the guardians in a position where they could no longer effectively guide this young man using the principles in which they believed.

David went home until September of that year, when his parents agreed to pay for him to go to a university. He applied to a prominent university and was accepted, but after only about three months of school, his grades deteriorated and he was very unhappy. He called his mother to complain about professors who were unfair with him. She agreed that he could come home, live there and go to a local college in order to get his grades up so that he could apply to another university. This he did and was accepted to his second university about a year later. After a few months the scenario repeated itself. In all he attended four universities without receiving a degree.

During all this time (six years) he was completely supported by his parents. Aged twenty-five, he gave up on school and went to work, as you might have guessed, for his father. By this time, alcohol had affected him significantly. His father made a job for him in his company for a year and a half and then simply had to let him go. David moved on to one job after another for the next five or six years.

It wasn't that he lacked talent. He had many opportunities with good companies and for short periods of time would impress his superiors, but as soon as he became comfortable in the firm he would once again act irresponsibly and be fired. David was married in his early thirties and unfortunately chose a woman who would drink with him and was considered the life of the party. His young wife was from a wealthy family that had spent a fortune on her education. She was a brilliant student who graduated with honors, but had also been raised in an indulgent environment.

David, with his well-ingrained habit of consistently looking to his parents, was not at all prepared to sustain the responsibility of marriage. Soon they were the parents of a son, but continued in the lifestyle to which they were accustomed. Jobs came and went with regularity.

Another child quickly arrived and the two children began life in a household run by totally different standards from those of David's parents a generation before. Incidents of marital discord became more and more frequent. Just as the two children were doing well at school, David and his wife decided to divorce. It was a messy breakup, and the wife gained custody of the two children.

David went on with his life, bouncing from job to job, borrowing money from his parents and continuing to allow alcohol to play a significant role in his life. Domestic discord plagued his family for many years.

I don't want to oversimplify this case by saying that one event that occurred when David was seventeen caused all of his troubles. Given the evidence, however, one must strongly consider that irresponsibility entered his life at that formative time.

I was a young man at the time, too, and I know that the events surrounding and following this incident strongly affected my beliefs about discipline, and the importance of assuming responsibility for one's actions.

A STORY

Margaret's Chore Chart

In August of 1999, I was in an American city, demonstrating my technique in a round pen, and during the intermission Jennifer Thompson came to me with her story. Two years had passed since we talked about the contract boards during a visit she made to Flag Is Up Farms, and she was eager to tell me just how well my system of contracts had worked with her daughter, Margaret.

Jennifer was a single parent. She was struggling to raise her daughter and was faced with the usual problems caused by a lack of structure, discipline, support and stability. She met Nolan, who had just lost his wife to cancer and was left with a daughter. Jennifer and Nolan were quick to get together, much to the surprise of Nolan's close friends, who found this new attachment, so soon after his wife's death, unacceptable. Nolan's daughter, however, was delighted with this new stepmother and the three of them quickly bonded. Nolan's daughter was a talented horsewoman, gifted with an innate ability to connect with these creatures of flight. It was because of her that the family had come to one of my demonstrations two years earlier. Tragedy was to strike yet again: Nolan's talented and lovely daughter was killed in a car accident. Within six months Nolan lost his whole family and found a new one.

Margaret was eight years old and going through some real growing pains. Nolan did not want to interfere, despite his experience of bringing up his daughter. He stayed out of the picture, hoping that Jennifer would sort out the problems she was facing. Their largest disagreements were over relatively minor chores such as brushing teeth, brushing hair, making the bed and doing homework. Margaret was also unreliable about the outside chores such as feeding the animals in the morning and evening, cleaning stalls and sweeping the barn.

Jennifer was at her wit's end when she visited me at the farm. I made suggestions to her about how to implement the blackboard system and on returning home Jennifer purchased dry-marker boards and special colored markers. Once the contracts had been agreed upon the new program commenced.

Margaret thrived under this new, agreement-based regime. She even reminded her mother when the contract needed to be updated, which surprised both Jennifer and Nolan. The "chore chart," as they called it, proved to be the answer to their dreams. They had spent a good deal of time setting it up so that it had no loopholes. Jennifer felt a huge sense of relief. It was as if the responsibility of punishment and argument was off her shoulders and they could get on with spending more "quality time," as she said, with Margaret.

They both found that suddenly their days were less disrupted and appeared to slow down. Margaret preferred activity involving genuine interaction with her family, with family-based rewards. It seemed as if they were suddenly learning a lot more about this child and her needs and desires. When in doubt about who should be doing a certain task, Margaret was asked to check the board. It was literally down in black and white. No excuses could be found for forgetting things or for noncompletion of duties.

As Margaret accepted the responsibility of commitment, they found their lives improved. Good time management hugely affects output, and a general feeling of achievement is a very positive thing. Peace and quiet further enhanced the feeling of harmony, and stress and tension were a thing of the past. Everyone benefited.

Jennifer adjusted the chart so that more and more difficult items were introduced, thus raising the bar on the positive side so that Margaret had more positive goals to reach for. This was stimulating for Margaret and greatly assisted the family in achieving a smooth-running home.

Jennifer was keen for me to include these details in my book. As she explained to me, it really does work. The mother-daughter relationship has gone full circle, from being very difficult to one that has surpassed their expectations.

Here is her chart:

RESPONSIBILITIES
A.M. Duties:
Brushing Teeth
Making Bed
Brushing Hair
Breakfast Duties
Getting Ready for School
Clean Stalls

Extras:
Laundry
Yard Work

NEGATIVES . . . IF NOT DONE
No allowance
No TV for the day
Do the dinner dishes

POSITIVE . . . IF DONE
$5 per week or $5 put in savings account
Pick a movie to watch with the family
Roller skating or quads [four-wheel drive, all-terrain vehicles]
Having a "me" day—choice of activity

Although I don't recommend money as a reward, Jennifer obviously used it successfully in this instance.

Jennifer Thompson is now applying this chore chart to her work in a nonprofit organization she has cofounded for a drug and alcohol outpatients' facility where she is an adolescent therapist.

A STORY

The Boy with Baggage

Over the years, my wife, Pat, and I have helped to raise about forty-seven "foster" children. They didn't come to us from official homes but from people who had heard that we were willing to take in kids—especially negative kids whom we were to try and turn around to a more positive way of thinking. We loved having them at Flag Is Up Farms, where they lived and often worked or apprenticed. We could support the children or young people in their endeavors to become truly valued members of society. Our contract system was constantly in use. Kids did well and it was acknowledged and they were rewarded. They did negative things and we handed out negative consequences.

A case that shows how a young person can be turned around by the contract system is that of Peter, who came to us as a foster child in the late 1960s. He was brought to my attention by a trainer at the Santa Anita racetrack in California. The trainer told me that Peter was a very small boy and at fourteen appeared to have the frame and stature to make a jockey. Peter had had a lot of trouble with the law and had been in and out of reform schools since about the age of ten.

Worse, Peter's parents were adults in crisis. They had both served jail sentences and abused drugs and alcohol. It was no surprise that Peter had a very bad attitude and was disrespectful to adults. At that particular time his father was in jail, but was very happy to find a home that would take Peter, as his life was on a collision course with disaster.

I had a couple of phone conversations with Peter's mother and each time she expressed a desire to find someone who would give Peter a chance. She was unable to control him and admitted she was now afraid of him. I spoke with Peter and I was intrigued that he seemed to be crying out for an opportunity to make something of himself. I agreed that the mother could bring him to the farm and that we could discuss the possibility of Peter becoming a foster child and, perhaps, training to be a jockey.

On the day that Peter and his mother arrived at Flag Is Up I greeted them and invited them to come into the house. As we crossed through the garage I heard a strange sound behind me, as if someone was dragging a chain. As I opened the kitchen door I motioned for both of them to go in ahead of me. The mother went in front and as Peter moved to go through the door, I heard this sound again. I looked down as Peter passed me. I was blown away by the fact that he had two chains, one around each ankle, dragging about six inches behind each foot. I came right out with it and asked, "What the heck is that all about with the chains?" Peter announced to me that he was a slave. "Slave," I said. "Who are you a slave to?" "Ahhhh! To my parents, and the cops mostly. I am also a slave to teachers and all that sort of thing." I remember standing in complete disbelief. I had not heard of this sort of fashion statement before and I don't think I have heard of it since.

I ushered them into the kitchen and introduced both the mother and Peter to Pat. While Pat was talking with them, I was able to get a good look at Peter and his mother. The mother was probably in her late thirties, but could have passed for fifty or even more. She looked hard and unkempt. Her facial skin was thick and revealed signs of severe acne. There was a large scar that traveled from just below her left ear to the left corner of her mouth. She was missing several teeth and spoke in a language nearly foreign to all except the street people around the suburbs of Los Angeles. Her clothes showed a lot of wear and desperately needed to visit a laundry. She stood about five four and was thin as a rail. I noticed tiny tattoos at the corners of her eyes, and a closer look revealed that they were in the shape of a tear drop.

Peter stood back from his mother and Pat, disassociating himself from the conversation. He was a rather normal young man in terms of his height, about five foot three, not unusual for a fourteen-year-old. He was very slight of build, however, and I noticed that his feet and hands were extremely small. Tiny feet and hands are probably the number one feature to note when assessing an early teenager for his potential to remain small enough to be a jockey as an adult.

Peter had black hair that was combed straight back on his head, with enough grease to take care of your car for a couple of months. The hair appeared not to have been washed for a significant period of time. He was dressed from top to bottom in black and everything on him was skin tight. He was a unique sight in the sixties and I had never seen anyone quite like him.

Peter's mother had a notarized letter from his father, which gave her full permission to make arrangements for Peter to live in a foster home and to enter into a program where he would receive instruction on being a jockey. It was clearly stated that the father was fully agreeable to any program within reason, so long as it didn't cost him a penny. At the conclusion of his time with us (at the age of eighteen), I would attempt to secure a position for Peter with a licensed trainer at a major racetrack. It would be up to Pat and me to make arrangements for his schooling and deal with teachers and administrators in the area of Peter's education.

I asked Peter to come with me on a brief tour of the farm. I probably needed to see somebody about something, but it was more to have time for a conversation with Peter than for any other reason. As we began to talk, I realized that I had an angry young man on my hands. Peter believed that the world was against him and that no one cared about his life. He had no respect for his parents and referred to them as criminals. He told me about their arrest records and also about crimes for which they were never arrested. His father, he said, was mean and vicious toward him, particularly if he had been drinking. Peter himself had been arrested many times. Because juvenile offenders were spared long jail terms his parents would send him to steal various items for them. He told me that he had probably engaged in theft close to a hundred times, but estimated that he had only been arrested seven or eight times.

I was intrigued and frightened at the same time. I felt anger toward the parents for what they had done to this young man, but I also had great concerns about bringing him into my operation and leaving myself vulnerable to a hardened criminal, even one of his young age. While driving around the farm we visited Al, my head rider at the time. I purposely arranged it so that Al could speak to Peter through the window of the pick-up truck, as I just didn't think it was time to get into conversation about why Peter dragged two chains behind him. Before going back to the house, we drove to the top of a nearby hill from where we could see the entire operation and talked over his dream to be a jockey.

Back at the house we sat down and outlined a rough draft agreement for Peter to live with us for the next four years. The mother agreed to each of the requests that Pat and I made and we agreed to hers. She only asked for visitation rights for both parents, for a brother and a sister from time to time and for Peter to go home at Christmas for a week or so, and a few days at Easter. We took two suitcases out of their car and his mother said goodbye. I remember that she walked over to Peter and put her hand on his shoulder, admonishing him to be a good boy. There was no hug or expression of affection. I took Peter to a room designated for him and asked him to remove his chains before going to the barn to report to Al, who would be in charge of him. He looked at me with a cold stare, as if reluctant to take them off, but without saying a word he removed them.

Peter, Al and I walked through the training barn, discussed the programs of a few horses and made arrangements to sit down with Peter that evening for an hour or so to discuss the future. Al and Peter got into a conversation while I was looking at a horse, and I recall a few comments that Peter made along the lines of "Nobody tells me what to do" and "I'm not going to be pushed around by anybody."

Our meeting that night was very interesting, and one that stands out as a memorable episode, even taking into consideration all the foster children we have had and the many incidents with which we have dealt.

Peter was damaged goods. He brought with him enough baggage for a forty-year-old, let alone a boy of fourteen. The one thing I remember that gave me great hope was that he was willing to talk about it. Once he trusted me, the stories started to roll out. He told how he was raped by a male reform school guard, about beatings at the hands of the police, and he described how his father procured customers for his mother's bed and how she entertained them virtually in the presence of him and his siblings. Outspoken about respecting no one and hating virtually everybody, he told us firmly that he felt a need to protect himself because he had no confidence that anybody else would.

Through this meeting I was able to collect enough information about Peter and his baggage to allow me to create contract boards that I felt would be effective for him.

The boards remained with Al and he gave me progress reports a couple of times a week, with recommendations based upon the results we were seeing. I created a "no options" board that included never stealing from anyone, and no drugs or alcohol. I included myself in these and agreed with Peter that we would never lie to each other. I found him to be a young man who enjoyed living up to his agreements, and as long as he understood what was expected of him, he was happy to work hard to comply. I also found him to be extremely quick of temper and vindictive if he felt that anyone had deceived him or acted against him in any way.

The contract board system worked perfectly for a young man of this mindset. I found that he had two great pleasures in his life: one was to go to the racetrack and the other was to ride off-road dirt bikes. He had ridden horses a little on a small farm just east of Los Angeles before coming to us and had driven minibikes on a course in the desert since about the age of nine. I set our agreements so that the positive consequences included taking him to the track and allowing him a morning at the stable area visiting jockeys and exercise riders and, when he was ready for it, even a mount every now and then. Though he enjoyed his time at the track, I think that driving the two hours there and back was probably most beneficial. I was able to outline for him all of the things I thought he could achieve in his life and conversely point out the potential pitfalls and their consequences.

Al helped him create a dirt-bike course in the riverbed just a mile or so from the training barn. Peter was in seventh heaven while riding there. One of the positive consequences on Peter's board was to receive a good mid-size dirt bike that for this young man was what a Rolls Royce would be to many people. Time in the riverbed with Al was precious to Peter and he would do extra things for Al and the horses in exchange for additional time on the course. It wasn't long before you didn't hear a negative word from Peter, because he felt it might cost him time at the track or on his river course.

Al and I simply stood back and allowed him the freedom to express himself, letting him take the consequences of any negative actions. We had to be objective and not interfere as he explored the contract system. He had discovered people who would stand behind their word and be as responsible as they wanted him to be; he, for his part, had been acquiring friends because other people saw him as positive and responsible. It seemed he was learning that if he trusted people, they would trust him. Classmates came to ride with him in the riverbed and I recall that some kids even made the trip up from the track to ride both horses and bikes. His grades improved, which was something none of us really expected, as Peter had a deep-seated hatred for schoolwork and figures of authority. Al had very cleverly woven into the fabric of the agreements incentives for his schoolwork to improve, and so it did.

Peter became a jockey. He wasn't a champion, but he performed very well. By the time he was eighteen, Peter was five feet seven and had to keep himself very thin in order to stay around the 115 pounds or so necessary to compete favorably. He eventually moved to training horses for racing.

We were able to seek out the inner triggers that could motivate this young man, so he was able to learn intrinsically. I cannot remember an occasion when Al or myself ever had a confrontation with Peter. I recall times when Peter lashed out at us verbally, explaining that he was not happy with something or other. Al and I kept our composure at every juncture and Peter's outbursts earned him negative consequences that were all part of the learning process.

I heard that his father died or was killed within a few months of the time that Peter came to us. His mother came back to visit two or three times, but it was never a significant factor in his growth; I don't remember that he visited his family for Christmas, Easter or any other time. Despite all that, he was able to move away from the negative influences of his life and to create for himself positive experiences that served him well.

Seven

CHOICE

Let them decide.

During Join-Up I never force the saddle or bridle on the horse. Instead, I provide an environment in which the horse willingly decides to allow himself to be saddled and eventually ridden. The horse takes responsibility for his actions and the whole process is more effective, more speedy and more positive than that used by traditional horsemen. Choice is equally as important to human beings, and to share with you my strong feeling that human beings need to be allowed freedom of choice so long as they are responsible for their own actions, I would like you to hear the story of Greg Ward.

GREG WARD

Greg was a major horse trainer for more than thirty years. He produced fourteen world champions and many millions of dollars' worth of high-quality horses that won competitions in show rings all over the world. Greg and I were university classmates in the late fifties. He came to college a very inexperienced horseman and I worked with him during his early days, because I had a good deal more experience in competition at that time. Greg was a deep thinker with an open and inquiring mind. I watched his progress over the years and was delighted to see him develop as a horseman to a world-class level.

In 1995 I visited Greg and his family on his farm in Tulare, California. I was interested to find that he and his son, John, have taken the concepts of nonconfrontational training to new territory. Greg told me that when he arrived at the decision to invite his young equine students to learn in an environment of complete freedom, his success level escalated appreciably. He gave them the freedom of choice. I felt that I had been doing a great service to young horses by releasing them in a round pen and allowing them to be responsible for their own actions, but controlling their direction within a matter of thirty minutes or so. By contrast, Greg allowed them twenty days of utter freedom to make their own choices.

The handlers of these young horses wouldn't even pull on the lead rope to get them to go in a particular direction. Instead, they would walk with them, encouraging them to go where they wanted, but never forcing. They were given the option to voluntarily make choices and be responsible for the consequences. Once the horses were saddled, the riders spent an hour or so in a controlled safe area, but never directed the horses in any way. They were free to go where they pleased. They would stop and eat; they might paw at the ground or even lie down; but they were never directed to fulfill the wishes of the rider.

Only after twenty days did these young horses receive direction from Greg Ward's handlers. If their choices were negative, the only discipline applied was to put them to work. They were given positive reward through rubbing, stroking and easing up on their workload. (By workload, I am referring to the schooling required for a horse to compete in Western show disciplines.)

The result of this radical departure from the traditional methods of training horses has been to create far more world-class competitors than Greg ever achieved previously.

•

Greg was diagnosed with cancer in March 1997, and from that time life was very difficult for him. His cancer was in advanced stages when discovered, and although extensive surgery prolonged his life, he immediately began to lose weight and strength. In the autumn of that year a crop of young horses bred within his facility took their first saddles, bridles and riders. Greg was drawn to a particular two-year-old colt right away and nicknamed him Magic. His official name was Reminic Pep, and Greg claimed him. "I want to win the World [Snaffle Bit Futurity Championship] once more," he said. Although he wasn't able to ride more than one horse per day, Magic was his choice. Through the spring of 1998 it became obvious that Reminic Pep was a very special young horse, but everyone around Greg wondered if his health would allow him to take part in the competition scheduled for late September in Fresno, California.

Greg did show Reminic Pep in the World Championship Snaffle Bit Futurity. (This involves reining maneuvers, working cattle out of the herd and working a cow down the fence, simulating what is required of the cattleman's horse.) He made the finals and won the championship on every judge's scorecard, twelve points clear of the second-place horse. This is a margin virtually unheard of in modern competition.

This is a story about a man who staved off death to accomplish a goal. In the year before the world championship Greg's weight had dropped below 100 pounds (from a normal of 170 or so). He appeared to be at death's door. The fact is, however, he managed to overcome his tremendous physical problems to compete against able-bodied young people in an event requiring an enormous amount of athletic skill. I don't believe that Greg Ward ever doubted for a minute that he and Magic would win that final contest. The fact is this was practically an impossible challenge to meet. And I don't know how he did it. But he did, and he triumphed.

He died on December 5, 1998, and will go down in the record books as one of the most successful Western horse trainers in history. Although his life is over, it is my hope that his life's work is far from finished. His son, John, and the young people whom he touched will hopefully carry on the studies that he began all those decades ago.

Greg was no psychologist, or even a student of the human mind. He was a horseman. But think for a moment about how his principles apply to people: violence and coercion simply do not educate effectively. People need to explore their own direction, make their own decisions and be guided by the consequences of their actions.

Throughout his working life, even in his own final personal achievement, he placed the idea of "choice" at the heart of his philosophy as a trainer—with extraordinary success.

Horses, these wonderful animals, brought their message to him and he proved that it works.

A STORY

Don't Judge a Book by Its Cover

Providing people with choices lies at the heart of my contract system. The freedom to choose also lies at the heart of the democratic system, the contrary of totalitarian regimes. The story of Jim Wood is a case in point.

Delbert Wood was my farm foreman back in the late sixties. You just couldn't fault Del; he was a valued team leader. He came to me one day and told me he was having problems with his son Jim and wanted to know if he could bring him to the farm to work for a while. Del figured that some quality time might just put things right. He assured me of his son's usefulness, and I was quick to approve the plan.

My first impression of the boy was anything but favorable. He was nineteen, about six feet tall and skinny as a rail. To my horror, half of that six feet was draped in hair. He had a ponytail he could put in his hip pocket. Up in his right ear was a series of earrings you could see a half mile away. I just went cold. First of all, you don't work around farm machinery with a long ponytail down your back. A ponytail caught in a feed chopper or a power takeoff unit can literally pull your head in and grind you up. Second, I couldn't handle seeing a young man with hair three feet long. Long hair on a man was much less acceptable in the sixties than it is today. I had a few conversations with Del about it, but we never came to any conclusions. Then Del suddenly died of a heart attack. Following his father's death Jim missed work for several days running.

When he returned I had words with him about his absence. He said he was devastated and he couldn't face coming to work, which was perfectly understandable. I began to wonder what on earth I was going to do with him. I was really concerned for his safety, and I went on to explain my doubts about his appearance. When I reached a decision about our working future I called him into my office.

"Jim," I said, "I don't want to let you go. You're a good worker, but I can't accept this long hair and earrings. I have decided to set up a contract with you. I am asking you to get your hair cut and to take your earrings out. I would like you to use all your talent to do the best job you can for me. As you work, you can let your hair grow again, if that is what you want. You can even put your earrings back in, so long as you are working well."

Jim agreed, we shook hands and he went to work. He worked like a trooper for five to six years. I watched him with pride. After about two or three months, his hair was getting a bit longer again. People would speculate, saying that they thought he would keep cutting his hair because he looked neat and everything was going well for him. Surely he would see the value of being more clean-cut. We all felt that he would leave the earrings at home as well.

I watched the hair keep growing until there was a little ponytail about an inch long. Then it was two inches long and the next thing you know there was one earring and then there were two and finally three. Within several months the ponytail was down to the middle of his back again. He was careful to put his hair out of the way when he was working around machinery. I never said a word about it.

One day he came to me and asked for a meeting. He outlined a plan he had for starting a business. He wanted to become a professional fence builder for the farms and ranches that were coming into the Santa Ynez Valley. I congratulated him and said that I would help in any way I could. He went off to create this company and it became a functioning, successful organization. He does a great job building fences, has a full crew working for him and owns lots of machinery. He is an extremely responsible businessman who lives up to his contracts, all done with his hair right down the middle of his back and earrings shining brightly.

Our contract opened the door to choice and Jim chose to work hard and earn his right to look and dress as he pleased. He chose to be responsible for his actions and I respected his choice.

In the late sixties Jim Wood taught me a lesson I should have learned as a child: don't judge a book by its cover. It is far better to judge someone by his actions than by his appearance. It is my hope that I helped Jim Wood learn something that assisted him, but I realize that he taught me a few things that are incredibly important.

CRAWFORD HALL

Some of the hardest choices have to be taken by those who, for whatever reason, lose physical mobility. I believe that only those who go through such trauma will ever really understand the difficulty of the decisions involved. Life as they have known it ceases and another type of life begins, one bereft of physical freedom but which can be both positive and challenging.

•

During World War II between the ages of seven and eleven I worked daily on my skills as a roper. I wanted to be proficient at this sport so that it would became an integral part of my horsemanship. These were lean years. We had no more students and a tiny horse facility. But the limitations of the time in fact gave me the chance I needed to refine my own skills. By about 1949 I was roping well enough to enter into competition with adults and I met Clarke Hall, a good roper willing to help me become a partner with him in *jack pot* roping throughout central California. His son, Crawford, then four or five years of age, was constantly around the arena and into everything as a child of that age often is. Crawford was riding horses at five and six years of age and grew up assisting his father on their ranch near Shandon, California.

I didn't see Crawford all that much during the fifties. I was then actively traveling to professional horse shows and rodeos throughout the country. Only in 1963 did Crawford come back into my life on a regular basis. By then Pat and I had settled in to our training operation near San Luis Obispo, about ten miles from California State Polytechnic University. Crawford had enrolled as a student there about four years after I left, and it was natural for Crawford to look us up.

Pat, our children and I all had a great time getting to know Crawford. He was an outright character. He was talented on a horse's back and had a keen interest in the psychological workings of the equine mind. When he completed his studies he went to work for his father in the ranching operations. It wasn't long before he came to the conclusion that horses held a great deal more interest for him than cattle ranching.

In 1973 Crawford went to work for my good friend Greg Ward. Greg was training both Western show horses and racehorses. Crawford was perfect for this job: he was talented with Western horses and light enough to ride racing prospects. Greg and I agreed that he was an up-and-coming talent in the world of horsemanship.

Then, in 1974 Crawford was in a freak riding accident that broke his neck and left him a quadriplegic. I was devastated by the news. When I visited him in the spinal injury unit he made it clear to me that if he couldn't continue to be connected with the horse industry, he simply didn't want to live.

On the drive home from the hospital my mind was working overtime on how I might help in some way. Flag Is Up Farms is virtually all on level ground and I concluded that it wouldn't be terribly difficult to set it up so that an electrically powered wheelchair could let him travel to virtually all of the areas where horse activities took place. It seemed to me that Crawford's eyes and brain could be a valuable asset to my operation, but it would have been very difficult for Greg to continue to use Crawford's talents.

Soon after, I began to work with medical staff in an effort to understand what we needed to do to execute such a plan. It was only a matter of weeks before a group of doctors requested a visit to Flag Is Up. But the doctors who came were not at all keen on our plan.

"It won't work," they said. "His condition is too fragile to allow him to perform the activities you have outlined. He no longer has a thermostat and so it will be very difficult for him to remain outdoors for extended periods of time. He will need far more rest time than other employees. The type of vehicles available will be hard-pressed to do the job. Since his life expectancy is presently three to five years we believe that you might lose him only shortly after he has acclimatized. We have programs for people with this problem that are far more effective than what you are offering him. It would be very difficult to execute the therapy necessary for Crawford if, at the same time, he was trying to do the work you've shown us he'd be handling."

This was a true setback, but I wasn't completely persuaded to give up. I discussed the situation with Pat, who encouraged me. "You have done a lot of things that most people thought were impossible," she told me. "Maybe you can do this, too." I called the doctors back the next day and simply said that I was going to follow through with the original plan. I notified Crawford and I could hear his excitement over the phone.

It wasn't long before he made the trip from Fresno to Flag Is Up Farms, in a van his family acquired for him, which had a hydraulic lift and the appropriate gear to accommodate his wheelchair. Crawford's family also financed a modular home fully equipped with all the necessary modifications for a quadriplegic. He finally moved onto the farm in late 1975.

There were glitches, to be sure, but within six months or so Crawford was rising to the task. He asked for, and I gave him, books and periodicals by the hundreds. He read voraciously, to become more proficient in the business of producing Thoroughbred racehorses. I remember it was within a year of Crawford arriving at Flag Is Up that I realized he was fully capable of taking over the management of the training facility. From the late seventies until the early nineties Crawford worked ten to fourteen hours a day, sometimes more. His physical condition aside, he was put to the test virtually every day in the same way that an able-bodied person might have been.

The doctors were amazed at the incredible speed with which Crawford became able to carry out his work. Few people even remembered that he was physically challenged. The doctors began to visit more regularly and soon asked if they could do a videotape about Crawford. I presumed they would show it to victims of spinal cord injuries as an illustration of how one person dealt with this catastrophe. I was surprised to learn it was not patients they had in mind as their target audience, but doctors and therapists whom they felt needed to change their minds about what quadriplegics are capable of doing. Recently Crawford took on the additional position of head instructor for the Monty Roberts International Learning Center and he regards it as a new and exciting challenge. He sometimes worries about teaching people when he is unable to demonstrate the activity in question, but students tell us that they learn more from him than from any fully mobile teacher they have ever had.

There are several important facets at work here. Motivation is clearly the food of life. I believe that if Crawford had not had this sort of activity available to him, he might not have lived past the three to five years that doctors said he had left. He's now been at the farm for twenty-five years. Instructing—his young horses, his riders or his more recent students—became a reason for him to exist. With each day, every new hurdle fueled his life.

Well-meaning people often say to me that I have been generous in giving Crawford this opportunity. The fact is, I have been on the receiving end of the partnership. I suppose, when you set out with intentions to do good things with your life, you often create circumstances that are good for you, too. I went into this circumstance expecting less than I was to give; it has actually worked out the other way around.

I can't remember a day when Crawford felt sorry for himself. His story should be an inspiration to all people, challenged or not. Your life is yours to develop and lead. You will get from it about what you are willing to put into it. Crawford's success reflects the depth of his wisdom and the fact that he recognized opportunities, not restrictions. Crawford Hall is in fact a model for the core principles of intrinsic motivation.

THE MUCKERS' STORY

I would like to relate to you a story about how allowing employees the freedom to choose a strategy, when accompanied by incentives and pride in their work, can result in a more successful solution than anything you can impose.

It all started when we began our operation on Flag Is Up in 1966. There were about seventy box stalls, and I was fully aware that cleaning the stalls and hauling the muck away was one of the most distasteful aspects of the entire horse industry. I had heard adults arguing over the problem from the time I was two or three years of age. I had witnessed many a good groom quit because he was sick and tired of mucking out stalls. I had observed countless talented riders leave the business entirely before agreeing to take on this most undesirable task. Over the decades owners and managers fired more help for problems involving mucking out than anything else.

I decided when I came to Flag Is Up that there would be a mucking crew. This crew would be equipped with a tractor and a large, state-of-the-art, hydraulically powered muck trailer. The trailer would be low-slung for ease of loading and it would have a large capacity to minimize the number of trips required in a working day. The crew would be made up of mucking specialists whom I would train myself, as I believed that I was one of the better stall muckers of my time. They would receive a bit more than the minimum wage and have a place to live. I would also keep an eye on their work and provide feedback and support for a job well done.

Everything progressed well in the first two years and we went from two to four men on the mucking crew with 130 stalls. I was pleased that the job was being done quite well and I had few problems. The system left riders to ride and grooms to groom and created a team of four men who were exceedingly proficient in mucking stalls.

One day my farm manager came to me and said that the mucking crew had requested a fifth man. I reluctantly agreed, but I informed him that this reduced their obligation from approximately thirty-five stalls each to twenty-six stalls, which seemed to me quite unnecessary. I asked my manager to point this out and indicate to the extended crew that I would like the stall mucking to be completed by nine in the morning. This meant that the training process could take place without interference from the mucking-out procedure, as the training barn would be completed by about seven in the morning, when the training began.

About two weeks later my farm manager returned once again. He told me that the crew had said that it was difficult to complete the cleaning by nine in the morning and that they required a sixth man. I was shocked and asked for a day or so to think this through.

I went away remembering that for years I had twenty-two stalls to clean each morning before school. My mind was filled with images of how I could muck and bed a stall in four or five minutes. I felt as though I needed to demonstrate this to the men so that they could understand how inappropriate it was to request the sixth man. A light came on in my brain. The next morning I went back to my manager and asked for a meeting with the crew that afternoon.

We met at the office of the training barn, and although my Spanish is more like "Spanglish," I felt I was reasonably eloquent in expressing my proposal. I told the team that I would clean and bed ten stalls. The men would time me. I would ask them to double the time that it took and to work out what their wage would be, given that amount of time. This would allow them to calculate the price per stall. I recall that it worked out to be sixty-two cents per stall. (Remember this was after *doubling* the time I took.) It seemed to me that this was fair and would allow them to complete their day at a more leisurely pace than my ten stalls. This price per stall would escalate with the national cost of living index, so as to take care of inflation.

The men stood in silence as I told them that we would meet the following day to discuss the proposal. That afternoon, however, my manager came to me and indicated that the men were waiting near their living quarters and they wanted another meeting. We drove there together and discovered that the team had chosen a spokesman who stepped forward to begin the negotiations. He explained to me that this proposal had created anger among some of the men and that most of them wanted to quit. He then asked me to walk through examples of what they would receive, given the number of stalls involved. I did that and I further outlined that this would be, in essence, their own business—they had the freedom to organize the mucking out as they saw fit. I added that the equipment would be their responsibility and they should maintain it as if it were their own. I would provide fuel. With these concepts in place I didn't care if they put on the sixth man or even the tenth man—they could have as much help as they wanted.

The following morning when I arrived at the training barn my foreman said that we had a serious situation regarding the mucking crew. He would meet with me round about midday to let me know what was taking place. I agreed and observed that there was an inordinate amount of activity and conversation taking place around the areas where the mucking crew was busy. I turned a blind eye and waited for the midday meeting.

My manager turned up in my office all smiles; our problems were over. He told me that the leader and one other man had decided that the two of them would take on the entire job. They intended to start at about three in the morning, which meant that they could finish with the training barn by about six-thirty, leaving the training hours free of any mucking crew. They would then do the breeding side of the farm and have it finished before noon. He went on to say that they had agreed to care for the equipment and keep it in tip-top shape. While minimum wage at that time would have earned a worker less than $500 a month, this system allowed for a grand total of $2600 a month allocated to the stall mucking. Since they decided that the two men would do all the work that meant that each would receive $1300 per month.

Mucking stalls instantly became a cherished position and not a distasteful job. I immediately noticed that these men were smiling and they took pride in their stalls and in their equipment.

No one ever knew when one of these men was going to take a vacation or was out with illness or for any other reason. They enrolled members of their families to replace them. The number of muckers has altered little over the years (from two to four) to meet the fluctuating workload. At no time, however, did I have to direct these changes; the men took care of it themselves.

I cannot remember dealing with a significant problem concerning stall mucking in these past thirty years. The two muckers we have today are related to the original ones and learned their skills from the generation before. The two muck trailers in use on our farm today are the original ones built in 1966.

Currently, two men clean an average of 150 stalls per day at Flag Is Up. The per stall fee is now $1.20. This may not seem a high income by today's standards, but it should be noted that these men normally have from three to five years of education. Their earning potential should compare to that of a fast-food worker or other minimum wage earner. A forty-hour week is equal to $840 a month on today's minimum wage standards and this is without housing and utilities. These men are earning approximately three times the national minimum wage. Most important, I am happy to pay it because it eliminates from my worries the most distasteful problem horsepeople have to deal with.

An interesting aside to this story has come to light over the years and serves to point out the innovative nature of people who are left alone to create an environment of success. Over the years the crew has chosen to go into one of the local villages and take a job at about ten dollars an hour, washing dishes for about two hours each evening. The additional twenty dollars a day means they are able to accumulate earnings of $2,500 per month, housing utilities included. Theirs has become one of the most productive positions for unskilled labor that I know of in the entire agricultural industry.

I gave the men a business, which they had freedom to administer themselves—they made their own decisions about how to organize it and distribute the money. Handing budgets over to people is a major part of decentralizing large companies and was used by Clive Warrilow at Volkswagen, North America. I applied the same principle, on a different scale, as we shall see in the next chapter.

Eight
CHANGE

*The carrot always works
better than the stick.*

THE ART OF LISTENING

When I step into the round pen to start a horse, I have a goal. I hope to elicit certain behavior changes from my "client," the horse. I do this not by insisting, threatening, intimidating or showing the horse who is "boss." Rather, I do a lot of listening; I watch closely what is happening with the horse and try to understand what the horse is experiencing. Psychologists call it "client-centered counseling." I remove the rope, and the horse is free to go away from me, or to move toward me. I set up a dialogue, and by understanding the horse's own goals, I am able to join him in achieving them. I ask the horse questions and wait to see what answers I receive. "You can decide what you want to do," I tell the horse. Through my body language I set up the possibility for a partnership and let the horse decide. I am a solid, steady, dependable center to which the horse can respond. I know the stages of the dialogue, and I watch for them to emerge. If I get resistance, I back off rather than make a big deal out of it. Resistance from the horse just tells me that I need to do something different, to change my own approach.

Equally, if a person is to change he must genuinely desire to transform his situation—genuine change cannot be imposed. Motivational interviewing—the equivalent of the dialogue I've developed with horses—can assist in giving people an intrinsic drive for change. I first heard about it from Dr. Bill (William R.) Miller, who initially developed this approach to work with people who have alcohol and other drug problems. It seems to evoke relatively rapid change. When he saw the film of my Join-Up with Shy Boy on public television, he recognized some striking similarities between his work with addictions and mine with horses, and he kindly sent me a copy of his book, coauthored by Dr. Stephen Rollnick, and training tapes. We later invited him to a clinic at the farm, where we discussed the similarities and differences in our approaches.

Motivational interviewing, Bill explained, began in 1982 when he was working with a group of newly trained psychologists at a hospital for alcoholism near Bergen, Norway. Over the course of six months, he demonstrated how he worked with people, and the young psychologists asked excellent questions that forced him to explain his rationale and methods.

His clinical approach emphasizes intrinsic motivation—listening for what is important to the person, and building motivation for change through the person's own values. His method provides the person with a lot of freedom and offers room for decision and choice. He asks open questions that allow for a wide variety of responses. For example, "In what way is that important to you?" rather than closed questions that have a short answer and often serve as roadblocks to communication, such as, "Is this or isn't this important to you?"

Change is precisely what I am asking of horses when they come into the round pen. I am asking them if they would like to Join-Up with the human race and accept the responsibility of a saddle, bridle and rider. The difference between my method and traditional methods of horse-breaking lies in the question, "Would you like to come and Join-Up with me?" I am offering my young horse the opportunity to change from being wild to becoming tame and a partner with a human being. The most important part of my technique is not the speed of that change (enormously useful as that is to trainers), but the fact that the horse makes a choice.

Years ago Americans with alcohol and other drug dependencies were treated in pretty much the same way as horses were traditionally. Horses were tied up and forced to submit to the trainer's will. They were given no choice in the matter, and if they balked, they were punished. Treatment for substance abuse was rather similar. The assumption was that alcoholics and drug addicts were slippery, cunning, lying, in denial and out of touch with reality. Within this belief system, the only effective way to treat alcoholics or addicts was to confront them harshly in order to "break down the walls of denial." This same language was used for horses—trainers broke them down in order to then build them up as they wanted them to be. There was no scientific evidence that this was the only effective way, either with alcoholics or with horses. It's just what people believed.

A theme running through such treatment is that "You have no choice" and "You cannot be in control." Choice and rational decisions were considered to be beyond the addict's capability. It was common to force people into treatment and to tell them what to do without much input from them. The goal of treatment was to break down the patient's ego. It was just one more example of a philosophy that almost always fails, and yet persists in society: if you can make them feel bad enough, then they will change. Social punishment and humiliation were used rather freely. Those who violated program rules might be forced to wear pajamas or an orange life jacket or a toilet seat around their necks. Heads were shaved. Therapy groups used a "hot seat" in which, one by one, participants were confronted, taunted, reminded of their failures and provoked—all in an effort to break them down.

Until recently, nobody believed that a horse is capable of conscious thought and decision. A horse, like an addict, was thought to be an irrational, mindless lower life form that required and deserved breaking. Like slaves, horses were offered no choices. I have clearly demonstrated that the horse is capable of conscious thought and therefore also of making choices and decisions. Join-Up respects this conscious thought and the horse's ability and right to decide.

People with alcohol and other drug problems are no less intelligent than other human beings. "You can't let them have a choice," some say, but the truth is that you can't ever remove that choice from them. They and only they ultimately decide to continue down the same road, or to take a new one. Of course, if you have a big enough stick you can force people (and horses) to do things. But pressure and abuse do not build strong people; they destroy good people. Only the very toughest, those with the highest self-esteem and sense of survival, make it back up again. It is not necessarily true that addicts are weak. My mother was a heavy drinker in later life, and I would never have said that she was a weak person. Her moral strength kept the entire family together. She was a wonderful support to me and tried hard to close the chasm between my father and me.

So if breaking people down isn't the best way to build them up, then what is the alternative? Over the years, enlightened people have put forward different, constructive approaches. My own work with horses is part of a larger, worldwide change to a better way of communication, one that is built on choice and trust, the essence of Join-Up.

One of the things that both Bill Miller and I recognize is the enormous importance of the spirit. When I take a raw young horse out into the round pen, I do not at any time want to break that horse's spirit. My intention instead is to join with that spirit, and to develop it to an even higher level. Without spirit, there is no responsibility, and without responsibility there are no decisions. The cultivated spirit is the cornerstone of growth.

As I read Bill's book, coauthored by Stephen Rollick, on motivational interviewing and watched his tapes, I realized I didn't need to memorize the details, because fundamentally we were doing the same thing. I immediately understood what I was seeing, even though I was watching a therapist and clients instead of a trainer and horses. The motivational interviewer does a lot of good listening, trying to understand and join with the client's own perspective. Instead of an interrogation, the questions are few and open-ended, giving the client lots of room to move. The interviewer is watching for signs of readiness, willingness to change, and reinforces them.

When encountering resistance, instead of blaming the client, the interviewer takes responsibility for it and gently backs off, looking for a better way to Join-Up. Ambivalence is seen as perfectly normal, not pathological. The therapist wants to understand the client's own concerns, goals, hopes and dreams. Any movement toward changing destructive habits is done within the context of what is important to the client. The interviewer helps the client resolve ambivalence in the direction of positive change.

When I start my horse in the round pen, I begin a conversation with that horse. With my body language, I ask open questions. These are questions that can illicit many different answers. I do not confront the horse or put him in a corner and whip him.

I watch, and no matter how the horse reacts, and every horse is different, I respond to the signs the horse gives me. As each horse is an individual, each horse is different; they all carry different baggage. Sometimes they move quickly toward the point of Join-Up; other times they do what people do when they are being ambiguous—they metaphorically sit on the fence. Those are the thinkers. You have to be very careful that the horse that does not move quickly through the phases of conversation to Join-Up is not blamed for being stubborn or resistant. Just like the addict who shows a conscious ambivalence to his or her situation, my horse is doing the same. Showing ambivalence is normal. It is part of the change process.

I keep up a constant flow of questions. I watch for the answers. When all my questions have been answered and the horse and I are ready, and not before, we go to the next phase. There is no coercion and no force. I listen reflectively and the horse speaks to me in his own language.

As I watched tapes of motivational interviewing, I saw the same thing happening. Alcoholics start to voice their own intelligent opinion about their present state of affairs and gradually begin moving in the direction of change. They don't need to be told they are doing wrong—they can see it for themselves if given support. There is no teaching going on here, but plenty of learning. The individuals begin to really see their situation, and what their options are. The horse in my round pen is disenchanted with running and is looking for a safe way to Join-Up with a new herd—the herd that I represent—just as the alcoholic or addict gets sick and tired of being sick and tired and looks for another way. The interviewer creates a safe place and offers the opportunity to Join-Up.

The language is different, of course, but the dialogue is virtually identical. Given room to move and some safe options, the human, like the horse, can make an intelligent, positive choice.

SLOW IS FAST

When educating horses there is no greater maxim than *slow is fast and fast is slow.* Rushing to get something done around a horse is the cause of many accidents. "Slow is fast" is an invaluable principle that can be applied to any situation.

Motivational interviewing taps into the core of people's desire to change, without using force or coercion. People suffering from addiction essentially learn about themselves. What is similar about my method of Join-Up is the speed at which this change occurs. I believe that the groundwork put into developing trust is always worth it, because once trust is established the learning process speeds up noticeably. I call this phenomenon "slow is fast."

During a question-and-answer session at one of my demonstrations, I was asked, "Mr. Roberts, we've been watching you and you're so patient. We can't muster that kind of patience. How do you do it?"

I asked, "Who is being patient?"

Traditionally, it takes four to six weeks to cause a horse to accept its first saddle and rider. If I can complete the task in just thirty minutes, then I believe I have the right to ask, "Who has patience, the traditional horseman or myself?"

The tortoise and hare fable still offers a useful lesson. I learned years ago that if you think you can complete a job in fifteen minutes, it's apt to take all day. If you work carefully as though you have got all day, it will often require only fifteen minutes.

I cannot stress enough the importance of this, both with horses and people. In working with Blushing ET, the horse that had an enormous problem with the starting gates, I found his fear of them was real and deep. I thought it might take a week or ten days at the outside to cure him of his phobia—it took me eighty days. This may seem a long time, but traditional methods had already failed and had only intensified his fear. By slowing every-thing down I got to the heart of his phobia.

Bob Clayton also understands that "slow is fast." He is now semiretired and working part-time as a telemarketer for a home improvement company. It is, he says, the hardest way to earn a living, with the possible exception of wrestling alligators. His job is to bother people via the telephone, between six-thirty and eight-thirty in the evening, when they are cooking, eating dinner, watching a favorite television program or are outside cutting the lawn, but are *not* interested in talking to someone on the phone about home improvements. In round-pen terms, he only has a few seconds in the ring. He says he has lost many good prospects by using traditional methods in an attempt to control potential clients. This includes talking fast and boring them with useless facts, upsetting their previous tranquillity. Watching Join-Up has taught him how to toss the line so prospects will know why he is calling, which causes them to circle around the ring. If the need for what he is offering is there, his prospect inadvertently lets him know with a remark here and there (similar to the ear, mouth and head action my horses communicate).

The success of his calls depends on creating enough trust to get a definite appointment (the joining-up) to allow a sales representative to give them a sales presentation (get ready for the saddle and mount) about their home improvement needs.

Another really important factor in the scenario of "slow is fast" is the importance of learning to control adrenaline. It requires intense concentration. I have taught myself over the years to control my pulse. The most nerve-racking situation with a horse will now simply trigger responses within me that lower my pulse rate. The horse is instinctively aware of this condition and will tend to synchronize with me. By doing this I convey a very important message to the horse, which is that there is nothing to worry about. Before a predator can attack its prey, it gets its heart racing, preparing to spring. By lowering my pulse rate, I am communicating the message that I am not predatorial. A horse will be alerted by a change in body language as the pulse rate rises and by a change in body odor. (It is said that animals can smell fear, and I have no doubt of it with horses.)

Adrenaline up, learning down; adrenaline down, learning up: it is a simple but priceless maxim.

When the boss tells you he has got five minutes to see you, you will probably enter his office with adrenaline in full flow, intent on getting your point over with one eye on the clock. If you enter his office relaxed and calm with no conscious thought about his tight schedule, you are more likely to be successful in your goal.

When I work with horses I know precisely how long I am taking to saddle, bridle and set a rider on the back of the horse, but I do not have any expectation of achieving my goal in a set time. "Slow is fast" is connected to another phenomenon, which I call *optimum learning*.

If you take the average speed of learning and you quantify it with a miles-per-hour number, then theoretically you might say that the average learning speed in the United States is fifty-five miles an hour. Having established that as a norm, we might be able to gauge that in Japan people operated at sixty-five miles an hour and in Germany it could be sixty-three.

Now, suppose somebody comes along and says that, given the right context, the learning rate could be raised to 100 miles per hour. If it is possible to learn at 100 miles per hour, then why is it that we accept a far slower learning rate? We have to ask how we can encourage students to learn at this higher rate and why it is that the majority of people learn at a speed that appears to be way below their optimum.

Optimum conditions are those in which the student can learn at speed. I use the term "optimum learning" to describe the ability to take on information, which, depending on the student's conditions or environment, can be absorbed at speeds that exceed normal expectations.

Trust is important in setting up the ideal environment for learning. It is established through conversation or communication, thus allowing needs to be assessed. The mutual understanding of needs establishes trust. Once the child, for example, understands that his needs will be met, he will be motivated to complete the job set out for him.

If the teacher or trainer listens and establishes trust, he is communicating with a deep level of commitment and caring. The problem is that few people are motivated to learn at capacity, and few teachers are motivated to teach at capacity.

Motivation is created when the means required to achieve a mutually desired goal are understood. "Dangling a carrot" provides the donkey with motivation to walk forward. We could push the donkey from behind (extrinsic) to get him to move, but that would be a tough job and would require excessive energy to achieve little, except perhaps resistance.

Motivation is imperative in the learning process. The horse sees that when he is circling the round pen he is isolated and so he works hard. I send him away to consider his options. In the natural world of the horse, cantering at the outer perimeter of the round pen is comparable to being sent away from the herd. The tendency of the castaway adolescent, for example, will be to circle the herd as the alpha female communicates to him that he is not welcome. She does this as discipline for an obstreperous act. The adolescent does feel isolated and tends to circle at speed hoping to find a way back in. Eventually, through communication, he is welcomed, but his behavior is subject to review and he may well be isolated once more. The horse makes a choice, and when he decides to Join-Up with me his work ceases. The very fact that the horse has chosen of his own free will to join my herd will motivate him to continue the relationship. He must then consider the options—work or accept saddle, bridle and rider. Once motivated, the horse will accept new challenges at an incredible speed. In the round pen I take a green, untried and unbroken horse to start, introducing it to saddle, bridle and rider in approximately thirty minutes. I have done 10,700-plus horses and that is the average time—some are faster and some take longer. Thirty minutes is what I would describe as the optimum learning speed.

The essential difference between traditional methods of learning and Join-Up is the context. The context of one is choice; the other is force. With both methods, the horse needs time to consider what has to be learned. In traditional training the horse is never quite convinced that you are a worthy leader of his herd. With Join-Up the horse becomes a willing partner and makes a conscious decision to follow the path of least resistance that I have created. I allow the horse the right to negotiate and discuss with me how he feels about this proposed partnership, so once he has made a decision, his ability to learn is unhindered by any fear of pain or force.

The instructor is not teaching but simply creating an environment for learning while staying out of the students' way, maximizing the chance for intrinsic learning to take place.

We slow the learning process down when we introduce fear, intimidation and misplaced consequences. When we give positive consequences for negative actions we derail the process of education to a significant degree; for example, if a student is allowed to disrupt the class because he or she is amusing. When the class responds with laughter the student is tacitly receiving positive reinforcement for his disruption. However, the class's approval is actually negative reinforcement (or positive reward for negative action), and it becomes responsible for slowing down learning.

Traditional horsemanship has for thousands of years been based on the precept of extrinsic motivation. The bit, the spur, the halter and the lead rope are all extrinsic forces. My method still uses extrinsic elements in the learning process, but my goal is to maximize the intrinsic and minimize the extrinsic motivation. My experience with foster children and my own biological children tells me that children are quite similar to horses in their desire to learn when intrinsically motivated.

The role of the teacher or trainer should be to encourage intrinsic learning, to encourage motivation. Extrinsic motivation is unlikely to produce a student able to exceed the teacher, but intrinsic motivation will often produce a student who surpasses the teacher.

When I began my college and university education in the mid-fifties I was entering the first generation of educated people who were instructed in great part by professor-written manuals, which were required reading. It was curious to me that certain professors would teach in an extrinsic fashion with these manuals, and others would stress intrinsic education.

My first year at university included a course in mathematics taught by Professor Boxer. At the same time I had a course in animal science taught by Professor Branham. Each of them had a course manual they had authored. Boxer outlined every issue and expected memorization. Branham, on the other hand, tended to give you the essence of each segment and requested you to use your brain and seek the answers. Memorization was replaced with innovation. Boxer tended to be stern and pedantic. He demanded absolute adherence to the road map to the answer. Branham was far more casual in his approach and was not concerned all that much with how you got the answer but that you eventually got it. I found students under Branham to be more content. They enjoyed the study more and I believe that the results of their study stayed with them through life. I feel that the Boxer model tends to leave the student shortly after the conclusion of the course. As I look back on the methodologies, it is clear that the instruction-based technique discouraged students from asking questions. On the other hand, some professors exposed the students to concepts that encouraged self-motivation. I was attracted to the latter approach and ultimately decided that these courses were the most interesting. The more open-ended the educational technique, the more it allowed me to get involved. I found myself going more often to professors who valued intrinsic motivation. I put forward theories and received information, and through this cross-flow of communication, I felt valued and trusted, as one should in an optimum learning environment.

When instructors assigned a series of statistics that I was to memorize, I was less inclined to take interest in the course and therefore the information made less of an impression. Information I gathered intrinsically, such as the lessons taught me by the wild horses on the Nevada desert, is still with me today. I believe that most students can trace the highs and the lows of their educational experiences by following a road map of their teachers' methodologies.

The principles of "slow is fast," adrenaline down and learning up, as well as intrinsic motivation, all create optimum learning. Change accepted from within will create an environment in which learning can take place at speed. I have proved it over and over again in my round pen and with the children Pat and I raised. Learning without pain or fear is the only path to follow.

A CORPORATE EXPERIENCE

Change and the Nature of Leadership

Since 1986 we have had many hundreds of corporations visit the farm and watch a horse being started. The corporate decision makers watch a Join-Up and I talk them through my concepts. I explain how communicating in the horse's own language establishes trust, and how, once we have trust, the whole process of learning is accelerated. I can see this strikes a chord. They then come to our home, have dinner and join in roundtable discussions regarding my methods. I have talked to literally thousands of executives over the years, so it was little surprise to me when I was contacted by Volkswagen of North America.

Volkswagen enjoyed a heyday in the mid-seventies. In the eighties, however, the upward spiral was reversed. An emergency call went out and Clive Warrilow was brought in from South Africa. He was to serve as a "paramedic" for a company in critical condition and became its president and CEO. Although I am keen to tell readers as much as possible about what Clive Warrilow did and the influence my techniques had on his decisions, it will be more direct if he tells the story himself.

What follows is based on a speech he made to the 1998 graduating class of the Business School of Oakland University.

My focus for tonight's address is . . . change and the nature of leadership today.

When I started out my business career in South Africa in 1963 working for Volkswagen, the very nature of business around the world was one of an autocratic management style. There was little regard for people or respect for their thoughts; management was somewhat by dictatorship and through intimidation.

Times have changed and people have learned, and now there's an understanding of the tremendous power that can be leveraged when everyone's individualism and creativity are unleashed.

We knew we had to change the way people thought

about themselves, their jobs, and how they worked—both as individuals and in teams.

The key question was: "How can you create a culture that values out-of-the-box thinking and participation when everyone is locked in a box on the corporate organization chart?"

Our greatest learning challenge was how to involve and engage all of our people in the business—setting them free to think and contribute. This is my most cherished leadership philosophy—set people free. To me, one of the greatest sins of management is to put people in boxes and keep them there. What a terrible waste for the organizations and what a lost chance for personal growth!

My philosophy is that in our private lives we deal with all sorts of challenges and opportunities. We make all sorts of decisions and by and large we make great progress. However, when we come to work, we are not asked to use our wisdom, intelligence, experience and leadership abilities, but just to do the job we are employed to do.

We believe in giving our people, or organization, a set of "tools" and core competencies that also break traditional paradigms. I don't know how many of you have read the article in the May edition of *Forbes* magazine about Monty Roberts, the horse trainer who wrote *The Man Who Listens to Horses*.

I had become acquainted with Monty Roberts shortly after coming to Volkswagen of America in 1994, and was truly inspired by the techniques he used—kindness and respect for the horses he trained rather than the traditional method of breaking the animal's spirit.

His basic philosophy was that the teacher must

create an environment in which the student can learn—
which is simple, direct and honest. A true life learning.
"You can't push information into an unwilling brain,"
says Monty. "There's no such thing as teaching. Only
learning."

The experience was so powerful for me . . . It fits
perfectly with the style of leadership that I had been experimenting with since the early eighties.

After our reorganization, I took our remaining executives back to Santa Barbara so they could experience
Monty's techniques and philosophy firsthand. As we all
walked single file around the training corral, I remember
hearing more than a few remarks and some mumbling
under the breath about "What are we doing here?" and
"Where are the cocktails?"

And then, people began to experience what Monty
Roberts could achieve with a horse that had never before
had a bridle, saddle and rider. This was not just about a
horse. It was a metaphor for a style of management that
says people will be better employees if you treat them
with dignity, respect and honesty. Trust goes a lot further
toward winning people over than ordering them around.

You, the graduating class of 1998, will be the leaders
of tomorrow. Your style of leadership will be one of the
most important choices you will make. No matter what
kind of organization you work for, whether hierarchi-
cal or flat, you will all have a personal measure of control over who you are and what sort of character you
embody.

At Volkswagen, we work very diligently to live by
these values: set people free—engage them—empower
them—motivate them—challenge them—help them to
learn.

I also believe that leaders must set and live the values of the organization. People are usually polite—they listen to what you say but then they watch what you do. It is vital for leaders to behave absolutely consistently between their words and their deeds. You can never earn the respect of your staff unless you walk the talk. I regularly tell our people that if I cannot earn their trust and respect, then I'll leave the company—to me, it's quite simple: Who follows a leader who cannot earn your trust and respect?

The other great learning of these past years has been the power of *focus* and *consistency*.

Focus on the things that make a difference and work on them as hard as you can.

Be consistent in everything you do—an organization gets quickly confused when the message and the direction change frequently.

As the leaders of tomorrow, if there is one thought I can leave you with, it is a quote from the Greek philosopher Plutarch: "The mind is not a vessel to be filled, but a fire to be lighted."

CONCLUSION

SIMPLICITY

*Before enlightenment you
chop wood and carry water;
after enlightenment you chop wood and carry water.*
—PROVERB

Many philosophers, scholars and teachers over the centuries have made similar reflections. It is the *real things* in life that matter. The elements of nature that sustain our lives will ultimately determine whether we have been a success or a failure. On our death beds it will not be technology or modern advances that will be foremost in our minds, but the touch of a loving hand, the image of a loyal companion or the memory of friends and family who have gone before, leaving fond memories.

The horse, an incredibly uncomplicated flight animal, can help us learn if we will but open our minds to the truth: genius lies in understanding the simplest things in life. I am often praised for discovering the concepts with which I work. In fact, I had to become simple to appreciate the values demonstrated to me by the flight animal.

I have often been alone with learned people, academics who could understand complex possibilities far beyond my field of vision. They were intrigued that I was able to cause animals to respond to me by communicating with them in their own language and impressed by the fact that I can ride a horse all day, always knowing my location, and the direction in which to return to camp, able to start a fire and cook a meal out there in the wilderness.

The hillbilly should never scoff at the young man who wants a higher education, but by the same token, the academic should not fail to see the value of the simple and natural. A person who has high goals should achieve an understanding of the natural and simple things of life, as well as the complicated and profound.

In order to achieve your goals in life, it is critically important to detach yourself from them. It is counterproductive to dwell on the outcome while in the act of pursuing it. If you believe that your direction is right, then working toward it will provide you with a successful outcome, within the appropriate time limits.

Horses have taught me to understand that if I set a target for a student but become obsessed only with the ultimate goal, I will fall short. On the other hand, if I work in the fashion that the horses have taught me, the goals will be met without force or pressure. Many years ago I concluded that I would detach myself from all outcome, almost as though I was a spectator. Although I was the architect of the work process, I never tried to teach horses but instead worked consistently to create an environment in which they could learn. I eventually discovered that many psychologists and psychiatrists recommended the same approach.

But the horses have been my teachers as much as I have been theirs. This may be a little like the chicken and egg as to whether humans or horses reached this point of understanding first, but I remind you that horses are 50 million years old, and human beings have been around for a much shorter period of time.

THE POWER OF GENTLENESS

Though I have earned a comprehensive academic education, the university context is not where I learned the principles I use in my hands-on work with horses. These wonderful animals were my teachers. I spent long hours with binoculars watching and learning about the nature, behavior and language of horses. I learned every detail and gradually translated it into a system of language and behavior that, coupled with my love for horses, formed the foundation for Join-Up. I am still learning, still discovering, still refining my approaches.

Books on management, human relationships in the workplace and related topics are plentiful these days. They are often full of good ideas and worthy of study. But if you are serious about using Join-Up in your company or organization, I encourage you to become a student of nature, a field researcher. It served me well, even as a boy.

Reapproach everything you know with wonder and curiosity. Study yourself, humans in general and then your work organization. Learn from people through observation and interaction. Learn to see; listen intently with your eyes and ears. Allow your mind to accept and receive messages you never realized existed.

Finally, if you want to pursue Join-Up as a concrete practice, you must give up what I call "the myth of the gentle." There is a prevailing, virtually worldwide belief that equates gentleness with weakness, slowness and lack of discipline.

When I stand in a round pen I am still and calm, supporting the horse even while it bucks and kicks in an effort to get the saddle off its back. I am calm because I have learned that any other state of mind is detrimental to Join-Up. Equus has taught me to remain calm in what may seem dangerous or difficult situations.

It is also *knowledge* that keeps me calm and free of any desire to dominate through fear. I am a willing partner to this horse, waiting for him to become a willing partner as well. Gentleness is the true strength of the world, not the threat and the whip. Violence always comes back in the form of more violence.

The exciting principle that I have been able to demonstrate, dramatically and consistently, is that gentleness, when exhibited as a set of carefully considered steps geared to the language of the other being, is the opposite of weakness. We are still fond of the notion that tough, aggressive heroes are really what we need, especially as leaders. I believe that Join-Up provides a different model, one that reveals the true power of gentleness.

It is my deepest wish that Join-Up and the gentler way will one day be accepted as truly revolutionary in both domains—the world of horses and the world of humans.

BIBLIOGRAPHY

Axtell, Roger E. *Gestures: The Do's and Taboos of Body Language Around the World*. New York: John Wiley & Sons Inc., 1991.

Burgoon, Judee K., David B. Buller, and W. Gill Woodall. *Nonverbal Communication: The Unspoken Dialogue*. New York: McGraw-Hill, 1996.

Davis, Stanley M., and Christopher Meyer. *Blur: The Speed of Change in the Connected Economy*. Reading, MA: Addison-Wesley, 1998.

Firestone, Robert W. *Compassionate Child-rearing: An In-Depth Approach to Optimal Parenting*. Cambridge, MA: Plenum Press, 1990.

Gibb, Jack. *Trust: A New Vision of Human Relationships for Business, Education, Family, and Personal Living*. North Hollywood, CA: Newcastle Publishing Co., 1991.

Gilligan, James, M.D. *Violence: Reflections on a National Epidemic*. New York: Vintage Books, 1991.

Goleman, Daniel. *Emotional Intelligence: Why It Can Matter More Than I.Q.* New York: Bantam Books, 1995.

Grandin, Temple. *Thinking in Pictures and Other Reports from My Life with Autism*. New York: Vintage Books, 1996.

Grandin, Temple, and M. Margaret Scariano. *Emergence, Labelled Autistic: A True Story*. New York: Warner Books, 1986.

Latham, Dr. Glenn I. *The Power of Positive Parenting*. Murray, UT: P & T Inc., 1990.

Masson, Jeffrey, and Susan McCarthy. *When Elephants Weep: The Emotional Lives of Animals*. New York: Delta Books, 1995.

Miller, William, and Stephen Rollnick. *Motivational Interviewing: Preparing People to Change Addictive Behavior*. New York: Guildford Press, 1991.

Appendices

Corporations That Have Visited Flag Is Up Farms

1989
ACCO International
  Corporation
Beckman Corporation
Beckman Instrument
  Corporation
Digital Equipment
Disney Corporation
Health Education's Technical
Kayadon Corporation
National Photo Finishers
Pillsbury Corporation
Santa Barbara County Schools
Searle Corporation
Security Pacific Bank
  Corporation
Spicer/Oppenheim
  Corporation
Syntax Corporation Probate
  Referee Association
Ventura School District

Young Presidents Organization

1990
American Academy of
  Pediatrics
Charter House Corporation
Conejo Valley School System
Cuna Corporation
Givenchy Corporation
Good Housekeeping
  Corporation
Harte Bank Corporation
I.C.I. Pharmaceutical
  Corporation
M.C.A. Corporation
Old Presidents' Organization
Pacific Dermatology
  Association
Santa Barbara County School
  System
Schering Corporation

Security Pacific Bank
Corporation

1991

Alexander Hamilton
Corporation
Century Company
Columbia Pictures
Dyntech Corporation Group
One
Dyntech Corporation Group
Two
I.C.E. Agricultural
Corporation
I.F.E. Corporation
John Hancock Financial
Services
Massachusetts Financial
Corporation
Mead Data Center
Metal Powders Industries
Miles Canada Corporation
National Pharmaceutical
Council
N.G.R. American Life
Corporation
Pacific Western Bank
Corporation
Prudential Bache Securities
Corporation
Sandoz Pharmaceutical
Corporation
Ticketmaster Corporation
W. E. Long Company

1992

Alpha Modular Group
Boehringer Ingleheim
Corporation
Borax Corporation

Century Company
Ciba-Geigy Corporation
Columbia Resources Group
Dillon Reed Corporation
Energy Investors Group
G.T.E. Corporation
Maagettigan/Phizer
Corporation
Massachusetts Financial
Corporation
Megan Porter Corporation
Miles Corporation
Price Waterhouse
Shearson-Lehman Corporation
Sungard Financial Group
Thomson Consumer
Electronics Corporation
Young Presidents'
Organization

1993

American Hospital Association
Bristol-Myers Corporation
Chrysler Presidents' Club
Ex-Ceed Motivation Trip
Flavors and Fragrance
Association
Fork UK Corporation
General American Life
Corporation
John Deere Corporation
Lexus Corporation
Malcolm Knapp Corporation
Merrill Lynch Corporation
N.A.A.D. Corporation
Oracle Corporation
Price Waterhouse Corporation
Prudential Bache Corporation
Retinel Advisory Committee
Rich Products Corporation

Riso Corporation
United Pacific Life
Wood Logan Corporation

1994
A.D.F. Achievers
Ameritas Life Insurance
AT&T Corporation
California Young Presidents
  Organization
Century Communication
  Corporation
Connor Clark Corporation
Dallas Sales Family Group
Disney Corporation
Fridas Corporation
G.I.H. Corporation
I.F.E. Corporation
La Salle Partners
Lennox Corporation
Oracle Corporation
Orthopedic Surgeons
Pioneer Hi Bred International
  Corporation
Price Waterhouse Corporation
Smith Barney Corporation
Smith Barney Shearson
  Corporation
Toyota Corporation
Visa Corporation
Volkswagen Corporation

1995
Adaptec Corporation
Advantage
Amgen
Blue Coral Corporation
Britannia
Citibank Corporation
Dain Bosworth

Dean Witter
Dr Pepper
4 Seasons
General Finance Corporation
General Refinancial
  Corporation
GM Canada
Guarantee Mutual
Hallmark Corporation
Hancock
Innovative Associates
Legent Corporation
Manu Life
National Reserve
Quaker Oats
Sara Lee
Smith Barney Corporation
Sutro
Syntax Corporation
Sysco
Ticor Agents
Visa Corporation
Warner Bros. Sales
Zerox Canada Corporation

1996
Chief Executives
Disney Corporation
Novo Corporation
Price Waterhouse
Texaco Corporation
Volkswagen National Press
  Conference
Warner Bros.

1997
Abbott Laboratories
Advest Inc.
Avon
Corning Ware Corporation

Dean Witter
Excel Industries
Federated Group
General Electric Corporation
Global Technology
Hoyts Corporation
Life Corporation
National Business Fellows
Nomads Corporation
Price Waterhouse
Professional Touch
PSMA Inc.
Reader's Digest
Senica Chemical Corporation
Sun America
Wynford Corporation

1998
Beaucom
Densply Corporation
Fox Corporation
General Dynamics Corporation
Innovation Network
Johnson & Johnson
    Corporation
Liberty Mutual Funds

Med Ed. Corporation
Morris Travel
Park Davisicuticals
Primedia
Prudential
US West
Washington Penn
    Insurance

1999
American Express
Ames Research
Beckman Instruments
BMW Corporation
Buick Corporation
Candle Corporation
CGEA
Exxon Corporation
GE Capital
Institutional Investors
Marketplace Media
MD Anderson
Penacor
Price Waterhouse Worlds
    President Org.
United Wisconsin

BLACKBOARDS

Example for children six years or under. The negative consequences, as well as the rewards, should be at the parent's discretion and of your own choice, depending on the parent, the child, lifestyle and geographic location.

POSITIVE BEHAVIOR

1. *Two full days without hitting brother or sister.*
   Trip to the park or zoo to see the animals.

2. *Two full days eating regular meals with good manners.*
   An appropriate educational movie, rented or theater, to be watched with parents.

3. *No disrespectful language directed toward a parent for two full days.*
   Parent will buy a book of your choice and read it to you.

NEGATIVE BEHAVIOR

1. *Hitting brother or sister anytime within two days.*
   Scrub four tiles in shower or bathroom area for two days.

2. *Failing to eat properly with good manners for two days.*
   One hour's work in garden or other place.

3. *Any disrespectful language toward parents for two full days.*
   Scrub kitchen floor (all or part, depending on the age of the child).

Example for teens.

POSITIVE BEHAVIOR

1. Clean up room each day for five-day period.
   A short trip outside the town with parents.

2. Homework well done and on time for one school week.
   A visit to the park or zoo with parents.

3. No bad language for one week.
   Good movie, rented or theater, to be watched with parents.

4. No displays of anger or violence for one full week.
   Shopping with parent for a desired piece of clothing or books.

5. An unexpectedly high grade in school.
   A party for all your friends.

NEGATIVE BEHAVIOR

1. *Untidy room through one week.*
   First clean room and then clean up garage or family room.

2. *Homework undone or late over a period of one week.*
   Write a page-long essay on responsibility and punctuality.

3. *Any bad language within one week.*
   Garden chores or cleaning the windows for one hour.

4. *Any displays of anger or violence within one week.*
   Clean bathroom in house and write a page-long essay on violence.

5. *A failing grade in school.*
   No evening privileges for two weeks, extra study time.

For Further Information

My goal is to leave the world a better place, for horses and people, than I found it.

In that effort I invite you to call for further information regarding clinics, conferences, educational videos and other products at:

on-line: www.montyroberts.com
e-mail: admin@montyroberts.com
phone: US code + 805 688 4264

Thank you,
 Monty Roberts